GW01090415

FROM WAR BABIES
TO GRANDMOTHERS

Forty-Eight Years in Psychoanalysis

Ilse Hellman

FROM WAR BABIES TO GRANDMOTHERS

Forty-Eight Years in Psychoanalysis

Ilse Hellman

Foreword by
Clifford Yorke

The Institute of Psycho-Analysis

London

1990

Karnac Books

London   New York

Acknowledgements

The author and publisher would like to thank *The International Journal of Psycho-Analysis, Psychoanalytic Study of the Child, The British Journal of Psychiatry, Bulletin of the Philadelphia Association for Psychoanalysis, Bulletin of the Hampstead Clinic,* Jason Aronson, and Pergamon Press for their permission to reprint some of the chapters in this volume.

First published in 1990 by
H. Karnac (Books) Ltd.
58 Gloucester Road
London SW7 4QY

Distributed in the United States of America by
Brunner/Mazel, Inc.
19 Union Square West
New York, NY 10003

Copyright © 1990
by Ilse Hellman

All rights reserved. No part of this book may be reproduced,
in any form, by any process or technique,
without the prior written permission of the publisher.

British Library Cataloguing in Publication Data
Hellman, Ilse
    From war babies to grandmothers: forty-eight years in psychoanalysis.
    1. Psychoanalysis — Biographies
    I. Title   II. Institute of Psychoanalysis
    150.19'5'0924

    ISBN 0-946439-66-4

Printed in Great Britain by BPCC Wheatons Ltd, Exeter

CONTENTS

FOREWORD

Clifford Yorke

Ilse Hellman's eightieth birthday was marked by celebrations at the British Psycho-Analytical Society and at the Anna Freud Centre in London. Analysts familiar with her work over the years, who have known her as analysands or supervisees or have otherwise been taught by her, and colleagues who have sat with her on various committees dealing with everything from training to administration had an opportunity to express their thoughts and feelings about her and the contributions she has made to her speciality over a busy and devoted professional lifetime. These tributes to the dedication of a lively and industrious mind, whose opinions and psychoanalytic thinking are firmly rooted in clinical experience, were necessarily restricted to a selected audience, though the interest in Ilse Hellman's work has a much more extended and international character. Her lectures, seminars, and contributions at scientific conferences in various parts of the world, including meetings of the Association of Child Psychoanalysis, as well as her publications, have called widespread attention to her work.

A colleague, Riccardo Steiner, had the happy idea that a wish to commemorate Ilse Hellman's eightieth birthday on a broader scale might well be expressed in a book that brought together some of the main streams of her contributions to child analysis. While many of us have cause to be grateful to her as an analyst of adults whose work was always informed by her deep understanding of normal and pathological child development, it is her work as a child analyst that has always called for particular study and attention. For her writings do not follow well-worn paths: the interests especially dear to her have led to studies unmatched in the rest of the literature on comparable subjects. The work on simultaneous analysis at the Anna Freud Centre, in which she has played such an active part, is unequalled in size and scope, though for reasons of confidentiality its representation has had to be somewhat restricted. The follow-up studies are unique. And the writings on adolescence, though devoted to a subject about which the literature is almost endless, show that individuality of thinking and presentation need not sacrifice any of the major psychoanalytic fundamentals established by Freud and built on by his daughter.

It may be of value to read these papers against a general background of Ilse Hellman's professional development; for this reason, the book opens with an interview, conducted by Riccardo Steiner, which provides the necessary setting for a fuller appreciation of her work. It would be wrong, however, to think that this book is designed only for those who work in a psychoanalytic ambience and have some acquaintance with the subject matter. It is hoped that newcomers to child analysis and workers in related fields—in education, nursery schools, dealing with the deprived, and the rapidly growing field of related specialities in social services—will find much to interest and even excite them in the pages that follow. It would be otiose to comment further on the range of interests unfolding through this book: nothing can be said that the author does not herself express better. It remains simply to say that this publication carries with it the affection of all who have known Ilse Hellman or have worked with her.

FROM WAR BABIES
TO GRANDMOTHERS

Forty-Eight Years in Psychoanalysis

My professional life

Ilse Hellman
interviewed by Riccardo Steiner

RICCARDO STEINER: As you know, the British Psychoanalytical Society is conducting interviews with distinguished psychoanalysts to place on record personal accounts of their professional lives. I wonder if you could tell us something about how you came to be interested in psychoanalysis, about the people you met and who influenced you.

ILSE HELLMAN: I wasn't an analyst in Vienna. I became an analyst here, in London. When I left school I was determined to learn about children, and that meant studying child psychology. I enrolled in what was then a famous two-year course on social work—one that specialized in juvenile delinquency. In the first year we learned the basics of social work. The second year was entirely devoted to practical work with children.

I don't know whether you ever heard of Judge Baker. He set up a foundation in America that did a great deal for juvenile delinquents who were taken away from home but

1

were too young to go to prison. So they had to be admitted to a home. The foundation opened a special home in France—the first of its kind in Europe. Two people came from France to Vienna to see whether, by any chance, there was anybody who knew French well enough to take a job there.

R.S.:   When was that?

I.H.:   That was in 1931. I was brought up to speak bi-lingually from the start, so French was just as easy to me as German. Much to my parents' horror, I decided to take the job and work in France. A colleague of mine, who had a French mother and had done the same diploma, came with me.

The home for delinquents was just about an hour away from Paris, and I stayed there two years. The children, who weren't criminals themselves, were children of fathers who were in prison or of emotionally disturbed mothers, some of them prostitutes, who couldn't look after them.

The home was a beautiful country house that some rich French people had given for the purpose. It was run on family lines, in groups, because it was thought, even in those days, that children who were away from their mothers needed to make firm attachments. So each staff member always looked after the same small group of children. That was how I started to work in the way that, some years later, was an integral part in the organization of the Anna Freud Wartime Nurseries.

While I was working at the home I started to study psychology at the Sorbonne. Evening classes were available, rather like those at Birkbeck College in London, and I did my first two years of psychology there.

I liked the home and would have liked to have stayed on in it, but I was transferred to Paris, to a Centre where we learnt to assess which families were so disturbed that their children had to be taken away from them. That turned out to be really interesting, and it didn't interfere at all with my University studies. But by the beginning of 1935 the French had already trained their own social workers and psychologists, so work permits were no longer given to Austrians, and we had to go home.

I returned to Vienna and at once went to the University, where there were two famous Professors of psychology, Carl Bühler and his wife Charlotte. She was the first professor to set up a Department of Child Development—no such thing existed in any other university in Europe. I had another year and a half to complete my course before I could take my degree; but Professor Bühler knew all the details of my work in Paris and allowed me to study while at the same time appointing me as a lecturer and research assistant. That was a great chance for me, because she was, at the time, making detailed studies of development in babies on the basis of meticulous and minute observations from birth onwards. These were the bases of her famous baby tests.

R.S.: I heard about that because the late Mrs Bick told me that she carried out her first baby observations at Charlotte Bühler's Institute. Could you say something about that?

I.H.: Esther Bick had become an assistant before me, but we were still together for nearly two years. The other assistant, who, like her, later became an analyst, was Dr Liselotte Frankl. She too was a lecturer when I went there.

R.S.: Could you tell us how these baby observations were carried out? I think it would interest all of us.

I.H.: We wanted to conduct observations from the moment of birth onwards, but it was very difficult to persuade the hospitals in Vienna to let students go there for this purpose. Luckily, we were given a chance to work in a large home for babies who were unwanted or neglected by their mothers. It was founded in the 1920s and exists to this day. The City of Vienna took these babies into this excellent home and encouraged research. We could choose whatever babies we wanted to study and spend as much time with them as we needed for our observations. We went in pairs: a child psychologist who was already knowledgeable and experienced was accompanied by a student. The psychologist would put into words what she saw, and the student would write it down. We all had to learn shorthand as fast as we could: there weren't any recording machines in those days! When I arrived there, I spent the first six months standing next to a research worker and writing down what she said she was observing.

There was also Hildegard Hetzer, who had worked with Charlotte Bühler in Germany. She joined her in Vienna, became associated with her work, and also became famous as a Professor of Child Development. Bühler's aim was to construct developmental profiles of children from the beginning of life by which monthly progress could be assessed and children compared with each other. For example, it was important to study the question of whether children who were consistently in contact with the same caretaker developed differently from children in Institutions, where the staff who took care of them repeatedly changed. Charlotte Bühler extended these studies into the sixth year of life, and my main work was involved with them.

R.S.:   While you were in Vienna at this time, did you have any contact with Anna Freud?

I.H.:   No, I never met her in Vienna, nor had I read much about psychoanalysis there. Charlotte Bühler was completely anti-psychoanalytic. All of us assistants were forbidden to go to listen to Anna Freud or to attend her seminars, although these were held only ten minutes' walk from the University. But quite a few people—Dr Emmy Sylvester, Dr Frankl and Esther Bick—went to them secretly. One of Professor Bühler's favourite sayings about the unconscious mind was that 'It's Mr Freud's and his daughter's fantasy, but it's not for me!'

R.S.:   It sounds rather like something that Piaget once said—that he never saw oedipal conflicts in his Institute! I remember hearing him say that.

I.H.:   I knew Piaget because he came to Vienna sometimes. He came to the same children's home to talk to the children, and we were repeatedly in touch with him. The first analyst I met and worked with in Vienna was René Spitz. He was so very interested in direct baby observation. I admired him and learned a great deal from him while he studied the 'smiling response.'

R.S.:   What brought you to England?

I.H.:   In 1935 Charlotte Bühler was invited to come to England as visiting Professor at University College, London, and she brought her first assistant, Dr Lotte Danzinger, with her. Cyril Burt played a big part in this. Miss Belle Rennie, who had seen some of her work in Vienna, set up a private child guidance clinic for Charlotte Bühler in London. She bought a house and paid for everything. It was called the Parents' Association Institute. In 1937 Professor Bühler asked me to join her. I was delighted because it was clear that the Nazis would soon be coming to Austria. Since 1934 their influence at the University was very strong, and tension among the students was constantly increasing. I thought it was an opportunity to get out. The assistant Charlotte Bühler had originally invited refused to leave. She was herself a leading Nazi and wanted, as she put it: 'to stay to see the Nazi sun rise over Austria.' So I was asked instead of her. That was in the summer of 1937.

Charlotte Bühler retained her post as Professor in Vienna, so she was only in London for about four months of the year. We used the Bühler tests mainly and worked with retarded children and sufferers from Down's Syndrome. We also worked with the parents and advised them about their children's difficulties. During Charlotte Bühler's absences in Vienna I was in charge of the Institute.

When I came to London, I met an analyst who played a very big part in my life and helped me a great deal. She was Susan Isaacs. She knew Charlotte Bühler's work and kept in touch with her in London; that was how we came to meet. At that time she answered letters to a weekly paper called the *Nursery World*. It still exists today and is concerned with the bringing up of young children. One of the reasons for its popularity was its answers to readers' questions—questions from mothers who were worried about their babies. At the time, Susan Isaacs answered them all, but the demand was far too much for her, and she asked me to help her. So every week I went to see her. We looked at the letters together; she gave me those she wanted me to answer and replied herself to the two or three most important ones, which would be printed. My own answers were sent direct to the mothers.

I thoroughly enjoyed my visits to her and learnt from her the way she approached child development and dealt with the difficulties of handling small children. Out of our meetings a friendship developed. It played a great part in my further studies and in my later work in her department at London University's Institute of Education.

R.S.:   What about psychoanalysis itself?

I.H.:   I still hadn't become involved in it. When the war broke out, the Buhler Institute was closed, because all children were evacuated from London. Charlotte Bühler herself went to America, and I was without a job. Child psychologists were needed to work in the evacuation service, so I joined the service from the outbreak of war. This meant that we were sent to places all over England where there were major problems. For instance, there were large numbers of bedwetters among the evacuees; homes for problem children had to be opened to cope with such difficulties, and child psychologists were needed to help.

I learnt a lot from these experiences. All these London children had been suddenly taken away from home. There had been major air raids in the East End. It was dangerous to sleep at home, and large numbers of people slept in the Underground stations. The schools usually organized the evacuations, and the children were sent to distant villages where it was hoped there would be no air raids. The people who lived in those places had no choice: billeting was obligatory, and they had to take a child whether they wanted to or not.

It may seem surprising, but many children had quite a good time and enjoyed the evacuation, at any rate to begin with. Still, they were separated from their parents, and when they were far from home they didn't see them for a very long time. Gradually, the childrens' disturbances, their anxieties, became sometimes very severe, and difficulties of all kinds became intensified. The foster families just weren't prepared for this and couldn't cope with it. Homes had to be set up by the local Councils.

When I came back to London, Gibraltar was evacuated: all the women and children came to London and were first put into hotels. That was at the beginning of 1941, and I had to help with the organization. But suddenly I got a letter from Anna Freud, who had heard about my work. I knew she had a Nursery in Wedderburn Road for about 20 children whose homes had been bombed and who had to be placed somewhere. She had been given money from America by the Foster Parents' Plan for War Children to open a bigger home in Netherhall Gardens. The new home could take 50 children, and she asked me if I would come to see the home and decide whether I would want to work there. Her letter was very amusing: she said she knew I had nothing to do with psychoanalysis but knew more about children in homes than most people. Perhaps I would like to spend a weekend in Wedderburn Road and see what I thought of it!

So I went there, and it seemed very strange to me. Naturally, the whole approach to children was based on psychoanalytic principles, and it was quite unlike anything I had seen before. The childrens' behaviour, and what was expected of them, was very different from other nurseries in terms of discipline and 'do's and don'ts'. I'll never forget when I first arrived. It was during the children's lunch-time, and all the one-and-a-half- to two-year-olds were eating with their hands. They sat around a big table, and they could choose what they wanted to eat. Usually in a childrens' home you put some food on a plate and tell them to eat up! But here there was a little buffet, and they could say what they wanted to eat, and if they didn't want it any more no one minded. When I was asked what it was like, I said, rather ironically: 'They ate spinach with their hands, and it looked rather peculiar, but maybe that makes one emotionally healthier!' It didn't make sense to me at the time, but it did when I thought about it later, because all the feeding disturbances I had seen in other homes didn't exist with children brought up like this. During my visit Anna Freud and Dorothy Burlingham talked to me about it all and asked me if I would like to come and work in the new house as a superintendent for the toddler department. At any rate, they suggested I should think it over. So I did just that, and accepted. The first children came in March, 1941, and I left in September, 1945, when the war ended.

R.S.:   When did you go into the analytic training?

I.H.:   Not straight away. But I got more and more interested through my contacts with Anna Freud. I saw her every day when she came to the Nursery; and she was marvellous with the children. She came at mealtimes, bathtime or bedtime, and simply to watch her talk to the children and to listen to the way she talked to all of us was lovely. The staff she chose were mainly young girls from Germany and Austria who had already had nursery-school training or, like Hansi Kennedy, who was 16 at the time, wanted to be trained as a nursery worker. (She later became a Director of the Anna Freud Centre.)

What appealed to me so much was Anna Freud's conviction that one couldn't bring up children who were separated from their families unless they became attached to someone, and that meant that the same staff members must always look after the same children. This had echoes of our work in Vienna and France. At the time, I think Anna Freud's was the only nursery where there was absolutely free access for mothers and fathers. In other nurseries there was a fixed visiting time of an hour or so once a week. Anna Freud's view was that only mothers who really wanted to keep a close relationship with their babies should be accepted, and they could come and go as they liked according to their working hours. So these children were not separated from their mothers as much as those in other nurseries, where the separation was sometimes so prolonged that the child didn't recognize his mother when he *did* see her.

The social workers who sent these children to us did so because they knew of our approach to these problems. Many of the mothers had illegitimate children, and many of them visited every day. Although they could have earned, and some did earn, a lot more money in munitions factories, many gave up their jobs to work in the nursery as kitchen staff or cleaners, so that they were in much closer touch with their children. That made a big difference to the whole development of these children.

Another idea that was new at the time and made sense to me was Anna Freud's recognition that the children couldn't be brought up without father substitutes. She was the first to recognize the importance of having men on the staff of the nursery. So we got conscientious objectors—they were all Quakers—young men who had refused to go to war and had been allowed to stay civilians on condition that they did hospital work or something helpful in connection with the war. (A third house was opened in the Essex countryside for the older children who didn't need to see their parents quite so much.) The homes were run in 'families', not only with substitute mothers but fathers as well to whom the children could get attached and with whom the boys could identify. The idea was adopted elsewhere and was a tremendous success. James Robertson was the Chief Social Worker at the time.

R.S.:   Had you decided by then to do the analytic training?

I.H.:   It was in my second year at the Nursery, in 1942, that Anna Freud said to me, just once or twice: 'Do you still find analysis strange? Wouldn't you like to become an analyst?' The person who played a big part in my decision to apply for the training was Dr Josefine Stross, the paediatrician who was responsible for our childrens' physical care. She had trained as an analyst in Austria. She suggested to me that it would be a good idea if I combined the training with my work at the Nursery. It was then that I began to read a lot and came to the conclusion that I really did want to train. But I had no money, because we were paid only two pounds, ten shillings a week, which was only just enough for our needs. Of course, we were living and eating in the Nursery, but you couldn't pay an analyst on what was left over.

It was then that Susan Isaacs inadvertently came to the rescue. She paid me for my work on the *Nursery World*. Anna Freud told me that one of her colleagues had heard that I wanted to start analysis and would take me for ten shillings a session. So I had two pounds ten from the Nursery, and the two pounds ten from Susan Isaacs paid for the analysis.

Then I applied to the Institute for training. The Institute was then in Gloucester Place, and my first interview was with Dr Edward Glover. That is not a very happy memory! He saw from my curriculum vitae that I had a degree in psychology from Vienna University and that I had worked with children all along. I have never forgotten his first question, which was: 'And what makes *you* think you'd be good as an analyst?' I found that a very difficult question. I explained that I did feel I could understand people's feelings and felt I could sense what they needed. 'And you think you can provide that?' he said. I thought I did rather badly because I got rather cross while I was listening to his questions. (Later I was told he was against accepting non-medical applicants at that particular time.)

The other analyst who interviewed me was Dr Sylvia Payne, who was totally different. She was very helpful and encouraging from the start. So I was accepted and started my analysis.

The whole training was very complicated, for two main reasons. One was the war. There were very few analysts in London—certainly few who could commit themselves in advance to a whole term's lectures. Many analysts had moved out of London, and many of the men, of course, were in the Army. But somehow or other, in spite of this, the training went on. The other problem, and one I found extremely confusing right from the beginning, was the difference in approach between Melanie Klein and Anna Freud. There were no 'groups' at the time, but different analysts gave very different types of lectures and seminars. My first patient, for example, was supervised by Anna Freud, but I had to present him in clinical seminars to Mrs Klein or Mrs Riviere. I felt I was told things that I was quite unable to understand, and I hadn't read enough yet to help me. So the same material was understood and interpreted quite differently by the different seminar leaders. As a beginner, I found this extremely confusing; but the person who rescued me was Sylvia Payne, who supervised my second case. Some time before, in her lectures, she had encouraged me to come and talk to her whenever I had any problems. I learned a great deal from her, especially about transference interpretations and the differences between the two theories and techniques.

The basic introductory course to Freud's thinking was taken by Dr Willi Hoffer, and I found it impressive, because his exposition of Freud's writings was so clear. I knew him well, so I could always ask him to clarify difficult points for me or ask him questions when I was confused about the differences between the ideas of various teachers.

R.S.:   Do you recall how Melanie Klein was teaching at that time?

I.H.:   Oh, yes. I had seminars with her, and my experiences with her were very nice. I knew, of course, that if I brought some material about my first patient, who was supervised by Anna Freud, that she saw things differently and would have dealt with the patient differently. But she didn't say, 'What you have done is wrong.' She had a very nice way of saying, 'Could one perhaps think that he might have meant something else?' She tried to minimize the feeling that what one was learning or what one was doing was no good. Many of her ideas were of course very interesting to me, since I had done so much work with babies and very small children. And there

was another, quite fortuitous, advantage in my relationship
with her. She got to know my husband, who was Professor of
History of Art—a subject in which she was very interested.
She and another analyst who was a Kleinian at the time—
Paula Heimann—knew a great deal about art, and they often
invited us. A relationship developed in which one could
easily ask questions about things one couldn't quite understand or quite accept. Although I found the training confusing at times, I did have the chance to talk things over with
senior people and get a lot of help.

R.S.:   And, of course, you also remember Winnicott?

I.H.:   I was interested in his ideas from the beginning. And
he was interested in the fact that I had worked in institutions
for so many years. He invited people to evenings in his own
home, held once a month, and I went there when I started
training in child analysis. Sometimes he brought his own
material, and he also asked others to bring theirs. So I took
mine, not only from my first case but also from the War
Nursery observations. We had fascinating discussions, but
at first I didn't find it easy to understand him, and he wasn't
good at explaining what he meant. But his wife Claire Winnicott was a wonderful help, and I was able to observe his
new ideas and watch them grow and develop for many years.

I think one of the most important changes that occurred
within the Institute came about when Paula Heimann left
the Kleinians. She talked and wrote a great deal about the
reasons why she couldn't follow certain of Mrs Klein's ideas
any longer. The people who were in close personal touch with
her were invited to come and discuss the change in her views,
but it was quite a problem for many. This happened when I
qualified in 1945. She was a great help to me at that time,
because when one qualifies and starts to work on one's own,
one usually needs advice from experienced colleagues. I
found her very supportive. Other colleagues who were particularly helpful to me then included Hedwig Hoffer, Dr
Hoffer's wife. She strongly believed that when one entered
private practice and first took cases without supervision, one

certainly needed help, and in 1946 she started a series of seminars for this purpose. Many of us went to her house once a week for midday meetings. We appreciated the time and thought she put into these meetings for people who were as yet quite inexperienced. These seminars played a big part in my work at the time.

R.S.: What did you feel about the Society once formal 'groups' had been set up? Did the division play a big part in political matters? What did you feel, for example, about the atmosphere in the 1960s?

I.H.: Before the groups were formed, students were very confused about what they were taught. This was particularly true about early child development. If you had no personal experience of little babies, it was even worse, because you had no basis on which to measure or assess the value of what you were told. There was considerable confusion between students who were in Kleinian analysis and those who weren't. My own feeling was that once groups were formed, it was some help. But it still wasn't easy. Those students who hadn't much experience with young children still faced the same difficulties: it is very hard, for example, to make up one's mind, on the basis of one's own observations, what babies might be thinking or feeling about the breast. At an early stage in training you hadn't yet analysed anybody, so you didn't have experience from which to draw conclusions. So many people had recourse mainly to reading. On the whole, I think the groups were of less help than might have been expected: you still had to be taught by representatives of each one and to try to evaluate their conflicting opinions on the basis of limited knowledge and experience.

R.S.: Can we turn to a more personal question? What do you think you have contributed to psychoanalysis as such? I ask you because you have published, for example, a few very important papers on simultaneous analysis.

I.H.: There were two main areas in which I got particularly interested. One was a research project, sponsored by the

Hampstead Clinic, on the simultaneous analysis of mothers and children. The basic idea came from Dorothy Burlingham, who had already worked on it in Austria. If, in the assessment of a child, it was found that the child needed analysis and that the mother too was very disturbed, one tried to encourage the mother as well as the child to have treatment. One analyst treated the child; another one treated the mother. Neither analyst knew what was happening in the treatment carried out by his colleague, but the treatment material from both analyses was made known to a third analyst, who was called the coordinator. The coordinator's job was to work out, as far as possible, the conscious and unconscious interactions between mother and child—to understand, for example, the impact of the mother's fantasies on the child's anxieties and disturbance. This procedure was followed with a number of cases and is still used to this day. I was responsible for the coordination of a number of cases; some were published, though for reasons of confidentiality not all of them could be. The ones I did publish were mainly concerned with children in adolescence or pre-adolescence. Among them was a boy who found the adolescent detachment from his mother unusually difficult, largely due to the fact that she felt unable to accept the detachment and became very depressed when she was threatened with it. That is just a brief example of the kind of work I was involved in.

Then Anna Freud wanted to set up an Adolescent Study Group and asked me to take charge of it. We met once a week over many years, and all students and staff who had adolescent cases came to the meetings and reported on their work with these children. Dr Liselotte Frankl and I published jointly a number of papers on adolescent development and related problems.

R.S.:   How did you find Anna Freud as a teacher?

I.H.:   Well, I experienced her as a teacher in a number of ways and in a number of different settings. For example, I was a pupil of hers when she still came to the Institute to give lectures and seminars. During the time of the air raids we had seminars in her house. The outstanding impression, and one that remains with me, was her capacity to register every detail of what was reported to her and form a clear picture of the patient. Anyone who has conducted a clinical seminar must know how difficult this is. Whenever I have been in this position I have found it very hard to know, from what the student has reported, whether I have an accurate picture of the patient or whether I have in some way distorted or added to what I have been told. With Anna Freud one always felt certain she had a clear picture. She always asked the relevant questions needed to complete the picture, and she would always point out to us those features of which we needed to take greater note or be more aware. That is a gift I have met in very few analysts. It was as if she had known the patient in person.

The other place where I learned so much from her was in the Nursery. On her daily visits she noted some of the difficulties the children presented; she listened to them, she watched them, she discussed them with all the people concerned with them, and gradually the problems became clearer as they unfolded. She had a great gift in her ability to make sense of what seemed at first incomprehensible.

R.S.:   Since those days you've contributed a lot to, and done a great deal for, the British Society. Could you say something about your later analytic career?

I.H.:   I was elected to full membership in 1952. In those days you could only become a member by reading a paper to the entire membership at a scientific meeting. You didn't have the comparative privacy of reading to a membership panel, and although people who have presented a membership paper in that way know how unnerving the experience can be, it still seems less traumatizing than the original procedure. They were helpful in the discussion, but not everyone made it easy for me, and at least one distinguished analyst gave me a rough time—though he wrote and apologized later. My paper was on migraine—like many so-called psychosomatic problems, an interesting subject for many analysts—and the meeting was very well attended, though papers for membership usually were.

In 1955 I became a training analyst. My sponsors were Michael Balint and Sylvia Payne then—neither of them members of my own group. Later I was allowed to do supervisions. I soon got my first training case, but it was interesting that several of the early candidates I analysed were Canadians. At that time there was no psychoanalytic institute in Canada, and many nationals from that country came to London to train. So I have many friends in the Canadian Society, and I keep in touch with them.

R.S.:   I have the impression that you got on well with members of other groups, as well as your own, from quite early days.

I.H.:   That is true. Fortunately, I was never one of those people who felt that disagreement in theoretical and clinical approaches was bound to lead to hostility. I was always on friendly terms with people who had very different ideas from my own, and that has helped to make my life in the British Society such an enjoyable one.

This may be one of the reasons why I have liked to serve on the various committees in the Institute and the Society. To enjoy committees you really have to be able to reach some accord with people with whom you might disagree on many important issues. In any case, I found the differences of view stimulating and at times even invigorating. One of the most enjoyable times I had was as Joint Secretary with Dr Rowley of the Training Committee. The job was arduous, because the Committee had not only to deal with interviewing applicants for training but also to devise the curriculum and deal with other permanent matters. The work was not divided up into sub-committees, as it is today. But, combined with my experience as a training analyst and as a teacher, it meant that I got to know students very well, and in later life this has been a source of great pleasure to me. Although I gave up accepting training cases for analysis when I reached 70, many of the analysts I trained and supervised come to see me and keep in close touch. It all makes my present life so nice.

R.S.:   Thank you very much, Dr Hellman.

PART ONE

The war nurseries
and follow-up studies

CHAPTER ONE

Work
in the Hampstead
War Nurseries

Although I knew Anna Freud for 42 years, I have chosen to speak only about a period during which we worked particularly closely together: the years from 1941 to 1945 in the Hampstead War Nurseries.

I met her first in 1940, soon after she opened the first War Nursery in Wedderburn Road. I was then working in the evacuation service helping to organize homes in various parts of the country for disturbed children who could not be settled in billets. I had not met her before and went to spend a weekend in the Nursery in order to learn about her approach, having worked for several years in children's institutions in France and Austria. She told me then that she and Dorothy Burlingham were planning to open two more Nurseries and asked me to come and work in Netherhall Gardens from

A version of this paper appeared in *The International Journal of Psycho-Analysis* (1983), 64:435–439.

1941 onwards. The American Foster Parents Plan for War Children were ready to finance these additional Nurseries, one in London and another in the country in Essex. I accepted with great interest, which grew still further with the opportunity, in the following months, to get to know more about the observations to be collected on the children and the plans for training the staff who would look after them.

In order to understand the thoughts Anna Freud and Mrs Burlingham had when they decided to open a residential nursery in 1940, it is best to recall their aims as they formulated them in their first publication, *Young Children in Wartime* (1942). They said: 'Our efforts are directed towards four main achievements:

1. To *repair* damage already caused by war conditions to the bodily and mental health of children. We therefore accept children who have suffered through bombing, shelter sleeping, indiscriminate evacuation, and billeting. We try to serve, on the one hand, as a convalescent home, and, on the other, whenever necessary, as a home for problem children.

2. To *prevent* further harm being done to the children. If small babies have to be separated from their mothers, we try to keep them in comparative safety within easy reach of their families. We provide every facility for visiting, so that the baby can develop an attachment for and knowledge of its mother and be prepared for a later return to normal family life. For the older children we make the necessary provision for ordinary peace-time education and, again, try to preserve the remnants of family attachments as far as possible.

3. *To do research* on the essential psychological needs of children: to study their reactions to bombing, destruction, and early separation from their families: to collect facts about the harmful consequences whenever their essential needs remain unsatisfied: to observe the general influence of community life at an early age on their development.

4. To instruct people interested in the forms of education based on psychological knowledge of the child; and

generally to work out a pattern of nursery life which can serve as a model for peace-time education in spite of the conditions of war. [pp. 11–12]

Research and training

Anna Freud had rightly anticipated that the first two aims of repairing and preventing damage had to over-ride the other aims under conditions of immediate danger and stress. It is for this reason that, however keen they were to use this opportunity for research, in order of precedence it had to be placed as the third, and teaching as the fourth, among their aims.

Throughout the years we were aware that we had a unique opportunity to collect longitudinal observations. The first part of the follow-up study of the children's development took place in our daily life with them. The paediatrician Dr Josefine Stross, who is a psychoanalyst, and all staff were trained to become observers under the guidance of Anna Freud. The method of pooling observations was used: it has since developed into an important research tool in psychoanalytic child observation. All members of staff, whether nurses, educators or students, were asked to write down observations they had made during their contacts with the children. These were to refer to all aspects of their behaviour, expected or unexpected, whether or not they confirmed or contradicted expectations. New steps forward or regressive moves, questions, fantasies and activities were noted.

A mass of observational material on each child thus became available. Meetings were used to classify and co-ordinate this material in order to fulfil the main aims: to form as complete a picture of each child as possible, its forward moves, existing problems and potential danger points. Attempts were made to understand his/her needs at any given time in order to meet them and facilitate the child's development. An attempt at cross-sectional pictures of children's reactions in comparison with the known developmental norms of those living under good family conditions were made. They centred on the problems arising from the disruption of family life, the reactions to partial separation from their mothers, their response to substitute mothering, to the effects of living in groups of contemporaries and the almost total absence of relationships to men.

It was clear from the beginning that Anna Freud's approach was based on her conviction of the pathogenic effect of children's separation from their mothers. It followed that a residential nursery had to provide conditions aimed at reducing this danger to a minimum. Very few people shared her view at the time. The evacuation of children from danger zones was a formidable task designed to save them from physical harm. The emotional danger resulting from separation from home and family was only gradually discovered.

Anna Freud's awareness of the likely consequences of the broken attachments led in the first place to the decision to give mothers free access to their children day and night, and to make it clear to them that we considered it most important that they make as much use as possible of this opportunity. Much work was needed to make some mothers feel that we really welcomed and wanted their visits. A number of them were delighted and took this unusual chance with enthusiasm, dropping in before and after work, coming at bedtime if possible, or in the early morning after having worked all night. The majority, however, had not foreseen this, either as their child's need or their own. Many were unable to make use of it for practical reasons; and for the children in the country house (who were older), such frequent visits could not, of course, be arranged. It is important to remember that, at the beginning of the war, there were no residential homes where the aim of keeping the ties to the parents unbroken was thought essential and where provisions were made for the necessary frequent contact. Some mothers, who felt that they wanted to be as close as possible to their children but could not provide a home for them, decided to give up their jobs and work in the nursery kitchens and other household departments, although they earned far less.

The second measure that was soon introduced was the provision of a substitute mother for each child. The need for children to have someone during the many hours and days when their own mothers were absent had quickly become clear. Observations of babies and toddlers, as well as older children straight after separation, showed that most of them spontaneously turned to a staff member, asking to be held, fed and played with, always by the same person. Each department got an experienced nurse or nursery worker as superintendent, according to the children's ages. In addition, a large number of young girls were taken on the staff. Most of them were untrained but eager to learn and ready to devote themselves to the multiple tasks required from a Mother Substitute. They did all the practical work for the physical care of the children and learned in the frequent meetings with Anna Freud and Mrs Burlingham, and in constant contact with the superintendents, what to observe in the children who were in their special care and in the others who shared their group life. The needs of each child were repeatedly discussed, with a view to finding ways of reducing the ill effects of separation and of overcoming existing problems. Miss Freud was always ready to listen and advise any nursery worker on ways to understand and to deal with a new problem, and she came to see the children at play, at meals and at bedtime.

Through the attachment to substitute mothers the children's development did not suffer the severe interferences that have since been studied in detail, yet the stability of the relationship, a 'trusting expectation', was not established. This was partly due to external factors, since such a relationship cannot be provided by staff whose own needs and changing plans have to be taken into account.

Relationship between mother and substitute mother

An important aspect was found to lie in the fact that a triangle was created. The effect of the mother's ambivalence towards the substitute mother, her admiration, jealousy and rivalry, the marked differences in her handling of the child in the substitute mother's presence or absence, the secrets kept from her, all had their repercussions on the children's character formation. Mother's and substitute mother's authority were played up against each other and they were used in turn to split the ambivalence. In this way certain features of an oedipal triangle became part of their experience, but with the anomaly of two female parent figures, which may have reinforced the male–female conflicts and their intensity.

The effects of these triangular relationships could be followed later in the analytic material of the few children who had analysis, relating especially to the time of separation from the substitute mother who, as the person who had 'abandoned' the child, became, for some time, the person on to whom all hate was concentrated.

The fact that these children were living with us because of the war, and that we lived under conditions of intense bombing in a background of constant preparedness for emergencies, might have led us to centre our interest on the children's reactions to these experiences rather than to the reactions to the absence of family life. Anna Freud made us aware of the importance of understanding that what they saw, heard and experienced of the war were not the main factors to influence their development. There was great variety in their responses according to their age, experience and their mother's capacity of dealing with the conditions the war imposed on them. We had for instance a considerable number of children who were with us, not because they had lost their homes, but because they had never had one. They had gone straight after birth from hospital to a shelter or foster home. They spent the first 4–5 years without the experience of family life. Others had had a short experience of a home of their own but had been to a succession of foster homes before coming to our Nursery. In order to understand, to some extent, what they might be feeling about the Nursery, it was of the greatest importance to try to reconstruct their past experiences by talking to their mothers. Those who had gone through bombing and had lost their fathers needed something more from us, especially during air raids, than those who were too young to understand intellectually what the danger was about and reacted mainly to the state of mind of the grownups who cared for them.

Most of the children had not grown up with a father; many had never known him. Observations of the reactions to this fact were discussed by Mrs Burlingham and Miss Freud in the book *Infants without Families* and in the 'Monthly Reports' sent to the American Foster Parents throughout the war and published in 1973 in the third volume of Anna Freud's *Collected Writings*.

The absence of the father in babyhood and in the oedipal phase, and the effect of this on their further development, was observed with regard to problems of identification, superego formation and object relations. In the seven cases where children had psychoanalytic treatment in later years, insight into the consequences of their fatherless upbringing could be traced into their adult life.

Miss Freud soon decided that men were needed as members of staff, and while it was impossible to provide each child with a substitute father, we were joined by six young conscientious objectors who were assigned to the London and Country Nurseries. They undertook the many necessary tasks of maintenance and gardening, and their presence brought an important contribution to the life and further development of boys and girls.

As one example of how some boys were affected, I want to bring observations concerning:

The role of the fantasy father

A father whose image was constantly alive in his son's mind was Bob's (from 2 years 8 months to 4 years 10 months). According to Bob, his father's feet were bigger than anyone else's; he could run 'faster than puffer trains'; and he could 'fly like a bird'. He had 'golden hair'. Bob's father was unknown and thus purely a product of his imagination.

Bob was born illegitimately. His mother boarded him out soon after birth; and up to the time of his entry into the Nursery he had lived in five foster homes and had rarely seen his mother. From then onwards she visited him regularly, and he grew very loving towards her.

He first mentioned his imaginary father at 2 years 8 months, when he cried for him in moments of despair. The next mention of his father occurred at 3 years 2 months, when he announced: 'My mummy and daddy are coming on Sunday'. He told everyone that his daddy had visited him in the Nursery and had bought him a toy car (which was in fact the possession of another child). Bob began to be very sensitive whenever he felt himself disbelieved. He asserted over and over again that his daddy was real, and he would sometimes stop in the middle of a game and shout, 'Yes. I do have a daddy!' though no one had at the time disputed it.

At 3 years 5 months his father image took a new and definite shape. Bob at this point went through a destructive stage and found it extremely difficult to curb his greed and to overcome his excessive and exhibitionistic masturbation. For the sake of his substitute mother he tried to cope with all these difficulties but failed over and over again and had many outbreaks of temper and despair. Whenever he did wrong, he explained, 'My daddy told me to', or 'My daddy likes it'.

At the age of 4 his father fantasy gave evidence of violently aggressive images within him. Talking about his 'family' he explained, 'I have got a new daddy. My uncle came and killed my daddy and my new daddy came and killed my uncle'. His father, he declared at the time, was dead. He had 'fallen out of an aeroplane. He was a bomb and he fell down and went all to pieces'. This was a time when Bob began to use swear words and instead of being affectionate towards his substitute mother, as before, he talked in an aggressive way.

A short time later the destructive father-fantasy and a fantasy of a Big Bobby who was *always* good became fused. The development of Bob's superego was expressed in the fact that his father never afterwards did anything that could be considered wrong. He became altogether strong, big and beautiful, and in the course of the next months (4½) took over the function of Bob's conscience.

Separation from the nursery and its traumatic effect

The experience of separation from the person who had played a central part in their early life presented itself differently in the children, according to the age at which they had entered Nursery life and in accordance with the nature of their attachment to the substitute mother and the real mother.

1. For those who had experienced life with their mothers before entering the Nursery and had lost the constant care of their mothers, the loss of the substitute mother was a repetition of the trauma they had experienced early on.
2. For those who had grown up in the Nursery from their early babyhood, the real mother had never been the central figure. The loss of the substitute mother was a first experience, and it coincided with the loss of the whole environment in which they had spent their early years. As was seen later in the analytic material and in real-life situations, the loss of the beautiful house they had lived in, of life among many contemporaries and especially of the benevolent adult world caused severe disruptions of development, leading to regression, depression and withdrawal, and to aggression and delinquent behaviour in several boys. Adaptation to rigid methods of discipline was impossible to accept for those who had grown up to latency in a non-punitive

environment, and therefore life in ordinary children's homes and schools brought many problems.

A systematic follow-up study of the children (now adults) has not been possible, but some have remained in touch with their substitute mothers, and we know about some aspects of the effect their war experiences have had on their later lives. Some of the comparisons of observations in their Nursery years and analytical material have been published in the *Psychoanalytic Study of the Child*.

CHAPTER TWO

Psychoanalytic material related to observations in early development

with Ivy Bennett

Early development

T he analysis of children whose early development has been followed by analytically trained observers provides us with opportunities for research of a special kind. Under ordinary circumstances we form our picture of the child's development and of the factors likely to have contributed to the establishment of his neurosis on the basis of the history obtained from the parents. In cases like the one to be presented here, circumstances have made it possible for one of the writers to be in daily contact with the child for a period of almost four years during his stay in a residential nursery in wartime.[1] Moreover, in his tenth year the child came into psychoanalytic treatment, and the writers have

A version of this paper appeared in *Psychoanalytic Study of the Child* (1951) 6:307–324.

been able to collaborate in comparing observations made during his early development with the material subsequently gained during his treatment. The relation between history and psychoanalytic insight can therefore be studied in greater detail and with greater precision than is possible in cases where we have to rely entirely on the parents' account. We can examine and verify how far certain early predictions we have made have in fact come true. We can follow the fate of the libidinal development, of the defenses and of early sublimations; we can see how permanent or passing object relationships have influenced the character formation; and we can gain greater insight into the relation between outer and inner reality by linking experiences the child has gone through under our eyes with the retrospective view we obtained about them in the course of analytic treatment. Finally, we may find that we have failed to observe, and therefore to counteract, certain trends that are shown to have played an important part in his later disturbance.

History before entering the Nursery

Martin has never seen his father. He is an illegitimate child, and his mother lived with him in a hostel until he was four months old, when he was weaned abruptly and placed in a foster family with eight other children. During this time his mother had to work and visited him on Sundays for a few hours. We know little about him until his admission to the Nursery, at the age of sixteen months, except that the foster home proved unsatisfactory. He had been confined to a cot most of the time and therefore did not learn to walk. He made no attempt to talk and became very subdued. For these reasons his mother removed him from the foster family, and he entered the Nursery.

In his first half-year, therefore, he has experienced sudden oral deprivation caused by rapid weaning and separation from an unusually loving and demonstrative mother. The effect of these severe early frustrations can clearly be traced throughout our observations. In addition, his early ego activities were greatly restricted owing to lack of space for free movement and lack of stimulus for intellectual and speech development.

The mother

Martin's mother is a country girl, and he was born in her middle twenties. She is tall, strong and heavily built and gives vent to her emotions freely. From the start she made it clear that she did not wish to talk about her past; she never referred to Martin's father, and her attitude was such that we did not attempt to broach the subject. She occasionally made derogatory remarks about men and was never seen in a man's company.

Whatever her feelings about the coming child may have been during her pregnancy, once Martin was born she grew extremely fond of him. In fact, her whole life came to centre around him, and under the most difficult wartime conditions she always found possibilities of providing him with every care. She made ample use of the opportunities the Nursery gave mothers to visit their children. She visited Martin daily, and after two years decided to join the Nursery staff in order to be with Martin always, although this meant a drastic reduction in her income. She often had sudden changes of mood and outbursts of temper but became so attached to the Nursery and especially to the superintendent of the department in which Martin lived that she has maintained a good relationship with her up to the present.

The Nursery

As has been described in detail elsewhere (Burlingham & A. Freud, 1944), the Nursery was so organized that each child belonged to a small 'family' of children under the care of a substitute mother. At twenty months Martin became very attached to the superintendent and for this reason was taken into her 'family' and spent most of his time with her while his mother was working. He formed a very good relationship with her and this has been maintained throughout subsequent years.

Observations during Martin's stay at the nursery

When Martin came to the Nursery at the age of sixteen months he was an unusually fat, placid baby, with bright blue eyes and long fair curls. He had great charm and caused much amusement from the start. After a few weeks of Nursery life, which gave him the freedom he had previously missed and reunited him with his mother, he began to walk and was generaly more active. His most remarkable characteristic was his greed. The sight of food excited him at any time of day, and he seemed insatiable. He was delighted with his mother's daily visits, which were mostly spent in kissing and cuddling. The mother stimulated him orally in an excessive way by giving him more sweets and food than even he demanded and by always kissing him on the mouth. It was typical of her sudden changes of mood that such demonstrations of love alternated with sudden outbursts of anger and smacking, only to end in reconciliation with once again renewed, prolonged kissing. These cycles, first observed in the second year, set the pattern for the intense sado-masochistic relationship that has had the most decisive influence on Martin's development.

Our observations during the second and third year centre mainly around the problem of his reluctance to give up immediate instinct gratification. In spite of his strong relationship with both his mother and his substitute mother, educational measures did not bring expected results. The modification of his instinctual demands proceeded extremely slowly. His greed persisted, his cleanliness training was not completed before his fifth year, he was unable to wait for satisfaction of any kind and seemed to adhere to the pleasure principle with unusual tenacity. Two main ways of evading demands could be observed: he would either make a humorous reply, act like a clown and make every effort to make us all laugh, or he would turn away from the person who had made the demand on him and turn towards another who did not know what had been expected of him. In this way he played up his mother against his substitute mother, and vice versa, successfully slipping between the attempts either of them had made to make him modify his behaviour. Martin usually seemed to be in a good mood, though not in any way overexcited or noisy. Most of his time was spent watching the adults at their work, pretending to work with them but in fact never carrying out an activity that needed any measure of concentration and perseverance. While watching or 'working' he usually sucked his thumb.

We watched Martin go through the oedipal phase without a father, and in his fourth year he appeared to take a turn towards masculinity in the manner usually observed with boys of his age. He insisted on wearing a cap or helmet, walked with long steps, talked in a deep voice and boasted of his strength. During this time he became very fond of a male worker in the Nursery, whom he imitated exactly. From his behaviour it was obvious that he not only loved him and wanted to become like him, but that in fantasy he really *was* 'Big Bill', and he referred to himself as 'a worker' in a nursery. After some time, however, it became apparent that this new development was not accompanied by the character changes usually connected with such a relationship. It seemed to be an 'as if' development, leaving his personality unchanged. His oral demands continued, and there was no trace of any successful beginnings of sublimation. Martin's language development continued to be very poor, and he never gave verbal expression to daydreams or fantasies. While most other children without fathers asked about them and told us elaborate fantasies concerning their fathers (Burlingham & A. Freud, 1944), Martin was never heard to refer to his. This must have been partly due to his mother's reticence about the subject, as well as to the fact that, unlike other mothers, she never confronted Martin with a man friend of hers. Treatment material later showed, however, that such fantasies were by no means lacking, and that it was the intensity and the terrifying nature of the child's inventions about the father that were responsible for his inability to express these early fantasies, and for his failure in making a complete masculine identification.

Martin went through a phase of great jealousy in relation to his substitute mother. Another boy, one year his senior, belonged to her 'family' of children in the Nursery, and during his fourth year Martin made great struggles to adjust himself to this rival's presence. He became more demanding and had temper tantrums when he felt unable to compete, or he uttered exaggerated boasts about his strength while avoiding competition in reality. He finally solved the situation by identification with the rival, referring to him as 'my twin' and demanding for him the same satisfaction as he himself expected.

Martin passed through a phase of pronounced exhibitionism and continuous boasting about the size of his 'willie'. When told on one occasion that he had good reason to be proud and that there was no need to reassure himself by keeping his 'willie' outside his trousers, he replied in the manner so typical of him: 'It isn't me who takes him out, it's he who is such a nosey fellow, and always wants to see what is going on,' forestalling in this way any criticism that might have been implied in the remark. During the same period his castration anxiety was intense and found direct expression in many ways; for example, one evening he had an erection in his bath and called his substitute mother in a panic, shouting 'My willie is coming off, come quickly.'

The mother continued to stimulate him physically, as she had done in his babyhood. She made a habit of asking him to her home for weekends, where he usually shared her bed. It was obvious that she derived a great deal of satisfaction from this close physical contact with him and that, in her refusal to have any sexual relationship with another man after

Martin's father, she used the child as an outlet for her sexual feelings.

As Martin approached the latency period, it became more and more apparent that certain essential features of normal development had failed to become established, and there were many reasons to foresee an unfavourable character formation. Our attempts to influence the mother had been unsuccessful. The educational influence of the Nursery staff and the opportunities provided in the Nursery setting for the development of sublimations in certain important directions had produced only superficial results. The tendency to evade demands persisted in his refusal to attend nursery school and was followed by truancy from school and failure to learn to read and write.

Observations after leaving the Nursery

When the war came to an end and the Nurseries were closed, Martin and his mother found it very difficult to part from what had been their home. Martin now had to attend the nearest elementary school in his district, and as this happened to be an old-fashioned, rigid school, which tried to impose discipline by punishment, Martin played truant, roamed the streets and became very aggressive towards his mother. He developed an eating disturbance during this period, which gave his mother great anxiety. As there seemed to be a great danger of a delinquent development, it was decided that Martin and his mother should go to live in a progressive school, where, as in the Nursery, she could work and he could take part in school activities.

After this change his behaviour improved, and his anxiety decreased before very long, but it very soon became apparent, as time went on, that Martin was unable to learn. At the age of nine he did not know any letters, was very poor in sums and although he had made a good beginning at handwork and games, he soon gave up all efforts when the task became too difficult for him.

The mother continued to let Martin sleep in her room, although she was repeatedly made aware of the unfavourable influence the sleeping arrangements were having on him, and despite the fact that the school provided opportunity for him to share a room with other boys.

At this point it was decided to arrange for Martin to have psychoanalytic treatment.

Treatment

Martin began his psychoanalytic treatment at the age of nine-and-a-half years. He is now a sturdy, handsome boy, with a shock of unruly blonde hair. He speaks in a soft, slow voice, and at times there is a delay, almost like thought blocking, in his answers, or he often seems to go into a daydream, leaving a sentence in midair.

He quickly understood the purpose of the treatment and admitted that he could not learn at school because he spent all his time daydreaming. He was ready to tell these daydreams but said, 'There are so many, it will take a whole year.'

Martin showed at once how fully absorbed he was by his relationship to his mother. The following example will illustrate how the pattern, established in his early years, has continued unchanged. He came one day very depressed and worried because his mother had threatened to kill herself by throwing herself under a bus.

> He elaborated fantasies of his mother being in hospital for two years with broken legs and himself having to push her in a wheel chair. He blamed himself for her desperation, because he could not read and was so naughty. He played sadistic games where the animals fought each other, biting and tasting each other's tails, or seizing and holding each other down with the mouth. A crocodile made a great bite in a mouse's tail and whirled it round and round until it was dizzy. Finally all the animals were

wounded, and they had to spend years in the hospital. Then Martin made all the animals kiss each other on the mouth and be friends again.

The next day he arrived saying, 'Instead of finding a dead mother, I had sweets and ice cream and went to the pictures with her.'

His first games soon developed into a picture of tremendous defenses maintained by a pose of superhuman strength, magic powers and a desperate denial and reversal of his fears. He would line up a colossal barricade of toys, while the therapist was allowed only a baby lamb or a milkmaid on her side. He was watchful and suspicious of every move her animals made and would pounce upon and squash them if they came on friendly visits. He did not lose his mistrust and suspicion of her until she played again and again the role he demanded, which was that she should be a wholly admiring and adoring mother who 'thinks her boy is marvellous' and who gives his exhibitions unqualified praise and admiration.

The beginning of Martin's analysis was made very difficult through three other features, whose interpretation he strongly resisted. First, he showed from the outset the force and stubbornness with which he sought to create a sadomasochistic relationship; he greatly enjoyed bargaining and attempting to provoke and bully the therapist into doing what he wanted, or tantalizing her in verbal play in which he always stopped at a significant point and mockingly refused to continue: '*That* I won't tell you', or '*That* I'll tell you next time.' Secondly, he also very cleverly used every opportunity to play off one adult against another, just as he had done throughout his years in the Nursery. Thirdly, his confusion between pretense and reality was so great that considerable time was necessary to make him aware of it. His acting and living in a world of pretense had worried his educators in his early years. The analysis now showed the degree to which he was dominated by these tendencies. The therapist appeared to be dangerous to Martin because she allowed him to express his wildest fantasies; and he was afraid he could do anything in her room—for example, kill her. 'You might say,' he said, 'or I might *pretend* you had said, that I should kill you—and I might do it before I knew I had been pretending you said I should.' He was afraid also that she would control his behaviour and *not* let him do things, or by magic power she would make him into a robot, who could not speak or walk.

Martin's reaction to transference interpretations was always to try to charm and cajole the therapist, in the greatest good humour, just as in his earlier years he used to make his mother and the Nursery staff laugh when they tried to win his co-operation. When these attempts failed, he reacted with what can only be described as a deluge of chaotic fantasies, which he dictated in the form of about 60 wild adventure stories. By this deluge any picture of the realities of his daily life was completely covered. This outpouring of unconscious material, the content of which could be understood and interpreted only at a later stage, brought him much relief. His fear of the analyst was interpreted, and positive transference feelings came into the foreground. The unusual richness of his fantasy productions contrasted sharply with the marked paucity of verbalized fantasy in Martin's infancy.

Three important themes from the material of the first year of Martin's treatment have been selected to illustrate the fate of developmental trends observed earlier in his childhood. These themes were: (1) the oral theme; (2) the father theme; and (3) the inhibition of looking, knowing and learning.

(1) *The oral theme.* In Martin's earliest animal games, the mouth played the leading role. Friendship, forgiveness, reconciliation of enemies, reunion with lost ones were all expressed by kissing on the mouth. This occurred between animals, between men and animals, and between man and boy. The mouth was likewise the chief organ of attack and destruction, and the animals bit and chewed, tasted, snapped and clutched at each other, or mauled and held each other down with the mouth. As treatment progressed, fantasies of

oral incorporation and destruction appeared in great profusion, expressed by drawings, vocal play and action. The following are typical of the many examples of this type of fantasy.

Martin drew a great bus, with many people in it, and a great fat man covering four seats. Another great fat man is on top of the bus; he reaches with his giant hand for the people sitting upstairs and eats them: 'You can see them going up his arm through the fingers and into the tummy, or into his mouth and down.' The giant is drawn spotted, and each spot stands for 3000 men he has eaten—his tummy is bursting full, but he eats those downstairs too.

He drew a 'sea enemy', which 'is bigger than a house.' It has great tentacles and sucks into itself houses, men and women. The people struggle and fight but get trapped and swallowed and come out dead by the big hole at the bottom.

Martin also revealed in a series of fantastic drawings his equation of the mouth and a vagina dentata. This was represented by a spiked starfish, giant's teeth or a crocodile savagely devouring snakes. The excessive oral stimulation and physical contact with his mother that Martin had experienced throughout and beyond the oedipal phase has led to fantasies of her as a sadistic, phallic mother, and any heterosexual fantasies about her can only be fraught with danger for his masculinity.

(2) *The father theme.* Martin showed his fantasies about his absent father, his feelings concerning the mystery surrounding him, and his profound longing for his return, in a series of stories dealing with dead men, corpses, secrets and a long-lost treasure.

His father came back in the guise of a soldier and was joyfully welcomed. He came back to an old ruined farm, which he made prosperous and thriving again. In the old farmhouse were thousands and thousands of dead men piled up in the attic, and all who came to search for the house's secrets were terrified and fled from the ghostly 'No–o–o–o–body kno–o–ows!'

The following example is chosen from this series to illustrate the horror and elaboration of Martin's fantasies:

In exploring the old house the discoverers had to use gas masks against a fierce bright light, which stung their eyes to tears. They found gold and diamonds and jewels and £50,000 on a silk cloth under each corpse. When the rows of dead men were struck on the head, jewels came out, not blood, but diamonds and gold stuffed in their heads and bodies. These men had died while trying to find the secret of the house—the house had 'doomed' them. It was a magic house, which got its own back on the invaders by flying away—the house and all the land it was on, the secret tunnels, dead men and jewels all went flying up in the air. The house warned the people inside to give up the search or it would dash itself and them to pieces. But the explorers attack, and see a great face flying in the air, big as a block of flats, a face like the ugliest man in the world. They shoot him in the eye and he falls dead. But the house continues flying and threatening and dares them to sleep or remain there overnight. They ignore this, and in the night the house makes a magic man, but they capture and shoot him. Then they get the idea and with great trouble burn the house, and what do they find? The house is a giant's head—they have been walking about and exploring for treasure in a giant's skull—or the inside of a big man's mouth.

Later stories showed that Martin's wish for his father's return was highly ambivalent, expressing Martin's oedipal jealousy and his fears about having to share his mother with a father rival.

The father returns, but he is both extremely aged and in some way impotent (i.e., he is a prisoner who has to be rescued, or is confined by a magic spell which he cannot break) and as soon as he establishes his identity, he immediately dies or is killed.

The next development of the father theme showed Martin's identification of his father with God and the link between his deeply hidden torment about his father's fate and his learning inhibition. Because he must not know the secret or understand the confusion about his father, he cannot know anything at all and completely fails to learn. He expressed his doubts and confusion about his father's death in the following fragment. Martin invented a village in Germany called 'God,' and here his favourite and invulnerable hero, Sailor Jim, met with many strange adventures. These reached a climax in a story that Martin concluded with tremendous speed and wealth of detail, as follows:

> Now Sailor Jim had a father—he was eight million thousand centuries old, and has just died today—No! he did not die, he was killed by somebody—we don't know who. They made a monument [Martin made a plasticine replica of Nelson's Column in Trafalgar Square] and put Sailor Jim's dead father on top. An ape-man who was 7000 years old [and had once been an ape but now grew to be so like a man that they let him out of the Zoo], the ape came and bowed to the monument and gave Sailor Jim messages from the father and told him there was a secret treasure under the old inn [God's Inn]. Sailor Jim put his soldiers on guard over the tomb, but the ape-man came out of a haunted house, eluded the guards and smashed up the statue and all the fence around it. No one heard him, and in the morning Sailor Jim came and saw the damage and wept!

> 'Who buried my father? Nobody knows!'
> 'Who killed my father? Nobody knows!'
> 'Who took him to his grave? Nobody knows!'
> 'Who buried him? Nobody knows!'
> 'He may still be alive.'

Sailor Jim hears voices that have come to haunt him, and he sends his soldiers everywhere shouting these questions, but every night the ape comes and smashes the tomb again. After many fights with the ape, Sailor Jim sees the tomb completely smashed by a madman, and out comes a big fat man. Sailor Jim runs and hugs and kisses him calling 'Father, Father.' The old man says he is 'only going to live for another 50,000 centuries' and goes off to live in God's Inn.

After Martin's fears and doubts about his father's existence or death had been discussed with him, the father theme developed in two new directions. First Martin related adventure stories about heroic Sailor Jim and his great friendship with wild animals.

'A very strong lion', for example, is Sailor Jim's 'one and only friend' who accompanies him on all his travels in the jungle, and several times when they are separated or the lion is lost, there always follows a joyful and lingering reunion over which Martin was several times very near to tears. There was also a crocodile, who calls 'Hello! Hello!' when Sailor Jim comes and they lick and kiss each other, because it is Sailor Jim's favourite crocodile.

It is clear that the wild animals (especially the lion) whom Sailor Jim has conciliated and whose ferocity is converted into special friendship, represent Martin's fantasy father, whom he has invented in his struggle to overcome his depression and the helpless confusion related to his father's absence and the mystery about him. His identification in fantasy with the powerful friendly animals indicates his attempt to create in imagination the father he has never known and by this means to borrow his strength, as well as to deny all castration dangers. In his reunion with the lion, Martin makes Sailor Jim act as if he had been punished and is now forgiven by his absent father.

Martin next told a story in which a crocodile eats a man all up, all except his little finger, which survives, floats on the river and multiplies into five fingers, which crawl up the bank and escape. This story opened the way for further interpretation of his castration fear, which markedly decreased his anxiety. Martin now allowed himself many fantasies and speculations about his mother's sexual life and the role his father must have played. He apparently had imagined that all the children in the Nursery were really his own brothers and sisters, and that his mother and father were really the parents of all the many coloured people and natives in his stories, 'who had been there ever since creation.' Martin had totally lacked any opportunity for real observation of his parents together but had made his observations upon courting couples in the park and now imagined episodes in which his therapist slept in a tent on Hampstead Heath.

The second new aspect of the father theme developed in a long series of fantasies of rivalry between two men in which fights went on ruthlessly and interminably and could never end because neither was allowed to win and the rivals fell dead simultaneously. When surprise was expressed at this invariable outcome and a query raised why it was impossible for either man to be allowed to win, Martin changed the form of his fantasy and acted out protracted struggles between a large and a small animal laced together by elastic bands in a tug-of-war that see-sawed across the table. After a heroic fight the baby lamb would succeed in pulling over the big horse, or the chickens would pull over the wild bull and lion. In many similar fantasies Martin expressed his intense rivalry with his father for his mother and his struggle against any man who came near her. He would not allow himself to win these battles, but neither would he allow the father rival to win, and the ensuing deadlock could only end in the death of both.

Martin also showed extreme degrees of jealousy and suspicion of his mother's activities, even going so far as to call upon the therapist late at night to check up on whether his mother had really visited her that evening.

Martin now began to express his thoughts about his mother's genitals and his ideas of a dangerous vagina dentata. His fantasies resembled the myth of the Medusa's head, the sight of which turned men to stone. His fears concerned a hidden penis (possibly the father's penis) which he believed to be in the woman's body and which would damage the man's penis when it entered her. To avoid these fantasy dangers he developed a hermaphrodite fantasy in which he was able to impregnate himself, like a terrible giant whom he drew with eleven large 'willies' from which he could sip lemonade whenever he wished. Martin stoutly asserted that there were women who had breasts *and* penises and quoted scientific books he had seen with pictures of hermaphrodites in them. According to his theory of how he was born, he was both his mother's husband and his own father. 'I just went to my mother and said "Can we be married?" and she said "Yes" '; so Martin and his mother had the baby Martin. He insisted he *was* her husband, and he dramatized pushing and shoving to get out of the womb.

Martin told the therapist that he had no secrets from her now, and he volunteered to tell all he really knew about his father. First his mother had told him that his father was a 'no-good Army bloke who was shot.' Later she told him this was all a lie, and she would tell him the truth when he was old enough. The therapist now asked if he did not think it would be better if he were told now. Martin answered very quickly 'Yes—now,' and asked her to discuss the matter with his mother. He was dejected at home and told his mother 'It's no good, Mum, the truth must come out, or Miss B. will guess it.' Then in a very difficult and emotional interview the mother told the therapist the whole story of Martin's father. She agreed that, with the help of the therapist, Martin should now be told the truth during treatment, and they discussed the best way of doing so. It was decided that the therapist should tell Martin that his mother was now willing to answer the most important questions that he wanted to know about his father.

The next day Martin came in a totally changed mood, very gay and affectionate and enormously relieved. He indicated the telling of secrets by drawing three men blowing great trumpets but did not yet want to tell anything he had learned.

In the following interviews he showed a marked change and considerably increased activity. Although not yet able to draw freely, he traced innumerable streamlined cars and aeroplanes, a horse's head and a large gun. These were in marked contrast to his first infantile scribbles and drawings of bodies with only head and legs.

The exploration and working through of the father theme resulted in a sudden spurt in Martin's masculine development. He has become decidedly more boyish and mature in manner and appearance. At school he has been made captain of his hockey team; he recently won the school's Junior Wrestling Championship; he has learned to ride a bicycle with skill. He said he never liked coming so much as since he started to draw cars, 'and I come early now, because I can come fast in light shoes.'

(3) *The inhibition of looking, knowing, and learning.* The third theme has been selected to show Martin's scopophilia, which, together with his oral aggressive fantasies and the taboo on knowing about his origins, resulted in his severe learning inhibition. This theme is richly interwoven with the fantasies about the father secret, and the first signs of freeing him from his inhibitions coincided exactly with his learning the truth about his father. Looking and being looked at played an important part in the treatment from the beginning. He told his mother that it was no good coming to see the therapist, because 'What good can it do just sitting there and looking at each other?' At this time he always gazed a long time into the therapist's eyes. One day he burst out with agitation: 'Don't look into my eyes like that.' When the projection was explained and his persistent looking into her eyes pointed out, Martin began to play frequent eyeing games and made magic gestures with his eyes and hands. He brought a torch and played it upon the therapist's face in the day in such a way that he could look at her unseen since the glare prevented her from seeing him. He would put the torch close to her eyes and dance about behind it, calling: 'Can you see me? Can you see me now?' At other times he played ghost games with the torch, putting it

below his chin, staring and calling in a low, moaning voice 'No eyes—no eyes!'

At this time Martin could not read at all and could write only his first name and the letter *B*. He now made a pair of huge, solid spectacles, like horse's blinkers, and held them over his eyes. He showed that he understood that the purpose of treatment was to remove the obstacles between him and learning, since 'not allowed to know' really meant 'unable to see, understand, being blind and therefore unable to learn.' When this was verbalized, he became obstinate and depressed and said he doubted whether he would ever be able to read. After he had gone, however, the therapist discovered that, under cover of the table, he had gouged holes through both sides of the blind spectacles.

Martin's various sexual observations in parks and in his mother's bedroom were discussed, and he demonstrated how his clandestine peeping had occurred. For example, he peeped at the therapist from behind a sheet of paper, or hid all of himself, except one eye, behind a door and peeped at her.

After a period of exhibitionism, which expressed his need for reassurance about his masculinity, Martin showed his sadistic conception of intercourse in which people kicked each other in the mouth. When this was discussed, he began to express fantasies about a terrible Medusa and the dangers of looking at her. He drew strange pre-historic creatures, which looked harmless but were really dangerous and had hundreds of snakes concealed in their feathers. Several times he said, 'See you next time, but only on television', indicating that direct looking was too dangerous for him. He related a story about a lovely young man with blue eyes who was turned into a fat creature with 25 arms and no eyes. He had only little dots instead and 'was really looking all the time, but he could not see with his little dots.'

Martin warned the therapist that if he went on coming to see her, '. . . we will come to the Ice Age—all the ice will come tumbling down, and you will be so frightened you will run away!' When this was interpreted as his own fear, Martin announced: 'So you mean my brains will grow? I'll be a boy! I'll help lots of people and do good in the world!' He said he wanted to publish a book and asked the therapist to help him. His ambition was also to be an actor, and he explained that an actor could arrange his life so that he was never alone—on the stage or backstage he could always have people laughing and liking him because he was such a gay, funny fellow. It was pointed out that he actually was never really able to *stop* acting or pretending; he had to clown and make jokes all the time, although one knew that he was sometimes very lonely and unhappy.

This interpretation was followed by a new flood of material showing his fantasies attached to numerals—as, for example, 2 was a man praying; 7 was a crutch or walking-stick; 3 was an acrobat lying on his back and holding another man on his hands; and 4 represented crossroads. Double digits represented combinations of images, such as 21, which meant 'A man kneeling down praying to his god; a very thin priest stands behind him saying "Shall I kill him now?" but he cannot kill him while he keeps praying'; or 8, 'Here are two cages and there is a bull in each and they are chasing each other fiercely in a never-ending race.'

The vivid fantasies condensed in the meaning which Martin attached to the numerals 1 to 100 were examined in detail, and two important new themes emerged in this material. One of these concerned fantasies of homosexual attack, and another contained the repetitive idea of 'a clown pretending to pray.' This latter image sums up the essential features of Martin's inner emotional situation and shows the combination of the mechanisms of clowning and pretense that were Martin's characteristic ways of dealing with his underlying depression and his fear of masculinity.

He also gave the meaning of the important letter *A*, which he saw as a pair of men's trousers through which he could look with X-ray eyes to the bones of the legs and feet and toes. He did not, however, 'see' the male genital through the trousers and was unable to draw the cross bar on the *A*. He began to allow himself to look at the shape of animals, which he traced from picture books with great concentration, and he showed with pride that he could read one word: 'Zoo.' The removal of the inhibition on looking was now indicated in drawings of a car with giant headlights on the front and rear, which were blazing in the surrounding dark, and searchlights on all sides, so that he could see attackers coming and 'see all there is to see in the landscape.'

Outcome of the first stage of treatment

Martin's treatment, as far as it has gone, has led to certain personality changes—in fact, to a marked change of mood and to increased activity. When the treatment began he was dominated by anxiety, suspicion, worry and depression. He covered these feelings by defenses of denial, reversal, exaggeration by number, clowning and a defensive use of humour. He has now become light-hearted, happy and busy, with a more genuine masculine development and a very much improved relationship with his mother and teachers. He is outstandingly successful in sports and has begun to make use of his intelligence in competition with other boys in drawing and parlour games. The discussion of the meaning of numerals was followed by Martin's first definite wish to learn, and his present sustained efforts in looking at details, e.g., of cars, planes, guns and horses. This can be taken to indicate that there is now a basis upon which systematic learning can soon be built.

Conclusions

The attempt to relate findings from psychoanalytic treatment to early observation in this case has brought a number of interesting points to light. It has, in effect, been possible to isolate and examine the fate, in later life, of some of the trends observed in Martin's early childhood during his residence in a wartime nursery.

(1)   Observations of boys who have grown up without a father have shown that they tend to create in imagination fantastically good and bad father figures. The fact that reality testing is impossible for them is a danger for their normal development. Normal masculine development is made very difficult for them by having no rival and therefore no object for identification. This is especially true in those cases where the mother has a hostile attitude to men. The friendly wild animals of Martin's fantasy show us how he created a father image, the positive aspect of which was a strong, protective and benevolent figure for whom he was an object of special tenderness and care. The negative aspect was evident in fantasies of a punitive and destructive father, e.g., in such images as that of a fierce giant who ate people.

(2)   The nature of his relationship to his mother, together with his homosexual fears and wishes about the fantasied return of the father, help us to understand the intensity of Martin's castration anxiety. The pattern of this relationship was established in the oral phase and was later carried over into an unconscious and mutual fantasy of being her husband. The near-realization of oedipal wishes made it essential to erect an incest barrier of special strength and at the same time heightened the fear of his father's wrath and retaliation, should he reappear.

(3)   In examining the records of his early years, it is striking how few of Martin's profuse fantasies were expressed either verbally or otherwise. The nature of his defenses seems to have made it more difficult than in the case of the other fatherless children in the Nursery to get insight into the fantasy life behind his placidity, laziness, clowning and good humour. The mother's personality, coupled with the fact that he spent weekends and other free time with her, away from the Nursery, further contributed to the difficulty of giving him more help through educational means. These two factors together, for example, have made it impossible to prevent Martin's looking and learning inhibition.

(4)   The predominance of the oral theme in Martin's material confirms our knowledge of the part played by sudden weaning and later oral overgratification in the development of a fixation on the oral level. He retained many personality characteristics of the oral phase, e.g., his greed, demandingness, overdependence and inability to wait for satisfactions. Moreover, the disturbance in the oral phase in Martin's development has been responsible for his difficulties in introjection and identification. In the nursery situation only the libidinal aspects of his oral tendencies were observable, whereas the oral sadism that played such an important part throughout his fantasy life remained hidden. His early exaggerated pleasures in eating (filling himself with good things) and in prolonged kissing with his mother may have served as defenses against his early oral–destructive fears and fantasies. This appears to have been the primary conflict behind his inability to incorporate. As far as the material has revealed at present, it seems highly probable that the elements that were involved in his difficulties on the oral level have contributed to his later failures in identification and his inability to take in through the eyes—an inability that formed the basis for his specific learning inhibition.

(5)   A child who has gone through the traumatic experience of sudden weaning coinciding with separation from his mother in his first year is disposed to react to later frustrations with excessive anxiety. The picture that Martin presents, of a child who is reluctant to give up the pleasure principle and consequently to change his behaviour for the sake of his love objects, can be understood as the outcome of his inability to bear painful tension or to master anxiety.

(6)   The danger of a delinquent character formation seemed to the observers to have been present from Martin's earliest years. The absence of a father, the interruption in the mother–child relationship and the inconsistency of the mother's handling were conditions unfavourable to normal character formation. In addition, the combination of a poor

ego endowment and barely average intelligence, together with strong instinctual urges, was considered to form the basis for an unfavourable prognosis. There were, moreover, certain early manifestations of delinquency, such as Martin's evasion of educational measures, his truancy from school and minor thefts from his mother. At the age of six to seven years overt delinquent trends were unmistakably present in his roaming the shops and streets while truanting. Martin, however, has not become a delinquent child, and there are several factors that may account for this. His relationship to his mother, although interrupted in the first half year, has not been broken, and she has always been basically a good and satisfying mother. This early relationship has made it possible for him to form strong and lasting attachments to other adults who have greatly influenced his character development. Martin's superego, for example, seems to have become effective through the influence of the Nursery, where educational methods favoured toleration and a very slow modification of instinctual urges. The special methods of the Nursery, the relationship with his substitute mother and the influence of the group all played their part in this process. They opened for him ways of meeting desirable standards without arousing excessive fear and guilt.

(7)   It has been found that in spite of close contact and a strong relationship extending over a long period, the educational setting could not influence, as favourably as we would have hoped, certain important trends of which we had long been aware in Martin's early development. Factors responsible for this seem to have been: (a) the severe traumatic experiences that took place within his first year, before Martin came to the Nursery (rapid weaning at four months, separation from his mother and frustration in a foster home at four to sixteen months); (b) the fact that the mother, while maintaining a friendly relationship with the Nursery staff, remained reticent about herself and consequently could not be influenced more than superficially in her handling of the boy; (c) the nature of Martin's defenses and his 'pretense' and

clowning behaviour have blurred the picture of his fantasies and his fundamental depression. In a later contribution, after the completion of Martin's analysis, it is hoped that the writers will be able to present further information about the fate of behaviour trends observed in his early life.

Cases in which long-term direct observation can be combined with analytic material open up possibilities for detailed study of important psychological and educational problems. Questions concerning the nature and extent of damage done by early separation, the conditions likely to counteract it, and the scope of remedial education in such cases can be investigated in this way.

NOTE

1. The Hampstead Nursery, London, which was organized by Dorothy Burlingham and Anna Freud. Miss I. Hellman was superintendent of the department for children from 18 months upwards.

CHAPTER THREE

Hampstead Nursery follow-up studies: sudden separation and its effect followed over twenty years

O bservational data recorded during war work with young children in the Hampstead Nurseries can now, twenty years later, serve as a basis for a small number of follow-up studies. Where follow-up contacts in later childhood and adolescence revealed problems for which psychoanalytic treatment seemed indicated, the children and their parents were informed of the opportunity for treatment at the Hampstead Child-Therapy Clinic. Only a few, however, have fully recognized their need and undertaken psychoanalysis. In these cases, the observations recorded in the Nursery and the subsequent analytic data provide rich

This paper forms part of a Research Project entitled 'Hampstead Nurseries Follow-up Study' conducted at the Hampstead Child-Therapy Clinic, London, and financed by the Ford Foundation, New York.

A version of this paper appeared in *Psychoanalytic Study of the Child* (1962), 17:159–174.

material for comparison and verification of the assumptions made earlier. Studies based on this material are now in their final stages, and papers dealing with the details of the findings are in preparation.

The Hampstead Follow-up Study has been concerned also with children whose development has proceeded satisfactorily and who have been able to deal with inner problems and external circumstances in ways that did not call for therapeutic intervention. The analytic material of these cases would have been of great interest for research, but the fact that these children were not in need of treatment has made it impossible to study their development by this method.

Without insight into unconscious processes, a long-term study of development is severely limited. Nevertheless, we have found that observations recorded over a period of years can lead to valuable conclusions if certain items found in early observations are followed and compared with subsequent observations made in direct contact with the children and their parents. The selection of trends that can be followed under these conditions needs careful consideration.

The following study of a girl, Jane, is based on such material. Jane was two years eight months when she entered the Hampstead Nursery and is now twenty-three years old.

Nature of observational data

The material used for this study differs in some important respects from material used in long-term studies elsewhere. In most other studies, the observations are planned with regard to frequency, time, place and circumstances under which they are made. While this procedure has the advantage of facilitating the systematic selection and comparison of data, it has the disadvantage that the data obtainable in planned situations contain only very limited aspects of the child's personality.

Our observations have not been collected according to a set plan. The common aim of observers in the Hampstead Nurseries was to record any item that seemed worth noting when it appeared to contribute to our knowledge of development, either confirming or contradicting expected reactions, bringing new points to our attention or helping towards a clearer understanding of an individual child. In our view, observations made in real life situations and by observers with whom the child has a relationship have a greater value than systematically collected data gained in set situations by neutral observers.

The child's spontaneous communications to people with whom he has a relationship permit insight into his emotional life as well as into fantasies related to the elaboration of past external experiences. His capacity to maintain object relationships over a long period and the nature of these object relationships can also be assessed.

In my role as 'substitute mother' during the years 1941–1945, I was able to observe Jane in the context of daily life. My observations were supplemented by other members of the Nursery staff who were well known to the child. Observations deriving from follow-up contacts through later childhood and adolescence into adult life were mainly made by me. One other observer who had also been on the Nursery staff and whom Jane had spontaneously contacted at the age of eleven, when she heard that the former Nursery worker was in the same town where she went to school, has contributed reports on her observations. While contacts during latency and adolescence were infrequent, they have become very frequent again during the last year.

While a variety of problems of child development can be followed up in this material, I have here centred my attention on the traumatic experience that this child went through in our presence and on the traces that her sudden separation from her mother left on her personality. For this reason, I have focussed on the relationship of her present personality to the very traumatic separation experience in her third year of life.

The Nursery setting

The Hampstead Nurseries were residential war nurseries organized by Anna Freud and Dorothy Burlingham and financed by the Foster Parents Plan, Inc., New York. Their aim was to provide comparative safety for young children whose mothers had decided against being evacuated with their children and who had to work in order to provide for themselves and their children. A large number of the children were fatherless. The Nurseries were planned in a way to reduce as far as possible the ill effects of separation. Parents had free access to their children, and each child was provided with a 'substitute mother' among the nursery staff. Each staff member had a 'family' of up to four children to look after. Although the children were in constant touch with all other children and staff in the house, they turned to their 'substitute mother' whenever they needed special attention.

Jane's development

Separation from mother

Jane entered the Hampstead Nursery under unusual and specially traumatic circumstances. She had not been prepared for the separation. She had come with her mother to accompany a friend who had arranged to bring her small boy, Bob, to the Nursery. Jane's mother decided on the spur of the moment, when she saw the Nursery, to ask if she could leave Jane there too. This was agreed to because war conditions had become very dangerous, and it was considered wise to accept Jane even though no preparation for this new situation had been possible. Jane had been born on the same day as Bob, in the same hospital ward, and it was hoped that the close friendship that existed between these mothers and children, who had met almost daily throughout their lives, would be a help in Jane's adjustment to the new place.

However, her reaction to the sudden separation was over-whelming. It has been described in the *Monthly Report of the Hampstead Nurseries* (August 1941) by Anna Freud and Dorothy Burlingham as follows:

> Jane was a gay and beautiful girl, well developed for her age. She was at first delighted with the new experience. When after several hours she understood that this meant separation from her mother, she broke down completely, cried incessantly and was hard to quiet. Frequent visits from the mother only seemed to aggravate this state. She formed apparently violent attachments with surprising quickness, but it took her a very long time to deal with the shock of separation.

Jane presented the picture of a child who had withdrawn her interest from the happenings around her. She spent much time sucking intensively, with a far-away look on her face.

She would often turn towards the wall and show little response to being talked to. During the first weeks, while her need to be close to one of the nurses was constant and still indiscriminate, she insisted on holding on and clinging to the nearest person. One of the nurses tied a skipping rope around her waist, which permitted her to use both hands for work. Jane was content when she could hold on to the handle of the rope.

In the *Annual Report of the Hampstead Nurseries* (1942), the authors described Jane's progress as follows:

> Jane was the child who took the longest time to adapt herself to nursery life. Her development was arrested through her concentration on her longing, her disappoint-ments and her varying moods of stubbornness and depres-sion. She entered in July and began at last to show signs of settling down about Christmas time. She began to transfer her affections, to be gay and to start all sorts of interests.

The observers who witnessed Jane's distress during the first days and weeks and her slow recovery during the first half year were much concerned with the long-term effect of this traumatic experience on the child. In order to mitigate the unfavourable consequences and to help the child back to normal functioning, Jane was provided with continuous substitute mothering by the adults of her own choice, and her mother was encouraged to visit whenever she was able to do so. She made ample use of this opportunity, and Jane was not in fact separated from her mother for more than two consecutive days during this stage. Bob remained Jane's close friend during their stay at the Nursery. His presence provided continuity, but Jane was always the leading partner in their relationship.

Research into the effects of separation shows that a great variety of inner and outer conditions must be taken into account in each individual case in order to evaluate the nature and degree of the ill effects on a child's further development: the age of the child; the nature of the mother–child relationship preceding the separation; the level of maturity reached by the child in the important aspects of his personality, i.e., his libidinal and aggressive development, his object relationships and the nature of his defenses. There are additional factors that have great influence on the child's potential recovery from the separation trauma: the substitute mothering that is offered and the way it is used by the child; the mother's reaction to the child's various manifestations of distress and anger and the mother's reaction to the child's attachment to the substitute mother. As far as they were open to direct observation, we have data on all these aspects of Jane's experiences that followed the shock of being left in the Nursery.

*Jane's history preceding entry
into the Hampstead Nursery*

The main facts about Jane's life and her development during the first two-and-a-half years were gradually pieced together from her mother's accounts and confirmed by the mother's friend who had known Jane from birth.

Jane was an illegitimate child. The mother was 29 years old when Jane was born. The father was a married man with whom Jane's mother had had a relationship for some time and of whom she was very fond. He took considerable interest in the baby, as his marriage had remained childless, and he continued to visit the mother and Jane and to support them financially until Jane was seven years old. Mother and child lived in a home for unmarried mothers during the first six weeks after leaving the hospital. They moved to a family where Jane's mother worked as domestic help. The mother said that she had never considered parting with her baby, and the absence of ambivalence was remarkable also in her subsequent relationship.

Jane was weaned at eight weeks, as the mother found that she could not go on with breast feeding when she started work. She was much concerned about this early weaning and later often talked about it with signs of guilt, once she knew that early weaning could have an unfavourable effect on children. From our later knowledge of the mother and her way of dealing with the child it was obvious that she had tried to compensate for breast feeding by much emphasis on food and sweets, the freedom to suck and a great deal of kissing. She derived much pleasure from making Jane look attractive and spent much time and thought on Jane's appearance.

It was also evident that the mother's determination to keep the baby with her at all costs and the fact that she was a very competent domestic worker had made it possible for her to find posts where she was allowed to have her baby with her, to look after her during her work and to have her sleep in her room. It is not known how many times the mother changed her employment during this phase; it appears that she changed posts at least twice, but that she never parted with Jane.

Physical development

According to the mother, Jane had been a large, well-developed, and attractive baby at birth and was much admired by nurses and other mothers. Her feeding was satisfactory, she had no illnesses, and she was described as well advanced and active compared with other babies.

Libidinal development

Jane's oral fixation was marked, and her intense need to suck and eat sweets was an important feature. She had also a great struggle to gain control over her bowel and bladder.

Ego development

Jane was described as alert and active, taking notice early, able to imitate movements and sounds and to say her first words early. All these memories about Jane's babyhood were reported by the mother on occasions when she compared her with babies whom she saw at the Hampstead Nursery. Her pride in Jane's good endowment was evident throughout, and it seems clear that Jane had been much stimulated by her. Stimulation had also come from the members of the families by whom Jane's mother was employed and whose household they shared. When Jane was admitted to the Nursery, her speech was well advanced, and so was her motor control.

The mother's personality

Jane's mother had herself been an illegitimate child and had been brought up in an institution. She sometimes spoke about her childhood in the convent, comparing the strict rules and deprivations with the free and satisfying nursery life at Hampstead. She was, however, very attached to the nuns who had brought her up, especially to the Mother Superior whom she still visited, and she expressed much gratitude for what they had done for her. This was later expressed also in her choice of school for Jane whom she wanted to be taught by nuns.

The mother's personality features that became known to us and that are likely to have had a favourable effect were the following. She had an excellent capacity to make and maintain relationships over a long time. Her friendship with Bob's mother has continued now for 23 years, she visits some of her former employers, has remained attached to the organizers of the Hampstead Nurseries and has always kept contact with me, turning to me for advice whenever she felt in need of it.

She is intelligent and very adaptable and showed a great capacity to learn. She was eager to understand the background of the educational methods used at the Nursery and has for many years consistently read the pages on child psychology that I wrote in a weekly paper for parents. She has attempted to modify her own approach to Jane accordingly and has lately been very successful in dealing with the problems of a stepson who was a disturbed institution child when she married his father.

Some unfavourable aspects of the mother's personality also became known to us. While the mother's capacity for forming and keeping relationships was remarkable, closer contact revealed antisocial character traits and delinquent tendencies. These manifested themselves in a number of situations in which 'outwitting other people in order to break rules' and especially to get more than her share played a part. Such 'successes' were related with obvious pride. All these incidents were connected with the wish to give Jane more than rationing would permit, especially where sweets and clothes were concerned.

During the second half of Jane's first year in the Nursery it became possible for the mother to join the household staff. This allowed her and Jane free access to each other as the mother worked in the house where Jane spent the greatest part of the day and where she slept. Both made ample use of this opportunity, but Jane's interest in activities in the Nursery School, which was in another house, was by then greater than the wish to stay with her mother, and she decided of her own accord to go out for the mornings. Her growing skills and her enjoyment of the nursery school were very marked, and the mother's encouragement and pride played a great part in this progress.

The vicissitudes of Jane's separation anxiety

From the second year of her stay in the Nursery onward, i.e., after she was four years old, Jane did not show extreme reactions to separations from her mother. She admitted that she missed her, was longing for her and was angry when the mother stayed away longer than Jane had expected her to do. Jane's relationship to her substitute mother and other members of staff were by then so well established that she felt free to talk about her feelings. She was one of the children best able to verbalize her thoughts and feelings, and it was clear that her capacity to express herself and to deal with ambivalent feelings against her mother in an open way were of the greatest help to her. This came to play an even greater part when, in her sixth year, war conditions made it necessary for the children to leave London and move to the country. This meant that Jane was for the first time separated from her mother for periods of one month, as visiting could not be arranged more frequently owing to distance and transport conditions. During the same period she was also separated from her substitute mother for a great part of each week.

During this phase Jane's thumb sucking at bedtime became intensified, and she regressed to bed wetting, from which she had not been consistently free for long. She never-

theless remained active and made great strides in sublimatory activities. She started school and learned eagerly and
well. She took part in many country activities that were new
to the child who had grown up in town.

Separation anxiety
manifested in relation to lost objects

During the second year of her stay in the Nursery, Jane went
through a phase of distress following the loss of her favourite
toy animal. She had become very attached to a toy cat, which
had been her constant companion. This was lost at the
cleaner's after Jane had had an infectious disease. When it
became clear that the cat could not be traced, Jane was
inconsolable, cried for it nightly and talked about it a great
deal in the daytime. It was obvious that this loss had revived
her distress at the time of the other separations. She did not
react to this loss by expressing her wish to be reunited,
because *she* felt the need for the comfort the cat had given
her; rather, all her feelings were expressed in terms of identification with it, sharing in fantasy the cat's feeling of being
lost. 'I keep thinking of the poor lost pussy, it looks at me with
its sad green eyes! It's far away from me and from all the
people who love it.'

The cat and its loss have remained fresh in Jane's
memory, while she cannot recall her arrival at the Nursery
or her distress about being left. She referred to the cat during
each of the follow-up visits. The facts themselves have
remained unaltered in her mind: 'Do you remember when my
dear pussy cat went to the cleaners and never came back?'
But gradually the theme of the lost animal became elaborated in her fantasy in the following way: during a visit at the
age of nine years, when Jane had again mentioned the inci-
dent, she told me later that she had decided on her future
career; she wanted to open and run a home for lost cats. This
was an elaborate plan, and her arguments ended with the

words: 'There should be no lost pussies in the world.' When the subject of her future career came up again a year later, Jane had decided to become a veterinary surgeon. This became even more realistic in the following year, when she won a scholarship to grammar school, which would allow her to go on to study at a university.

Throughout the years when the fantasy about the home for lost cats and later the wish to become a veterinary surgeon were in the foreground, Jane spent much of her free time looking after cats and other pets with much kindness and the competence that is typical of her and her mother.

A year later Jane had changed her mind about her future career. She said to me: 'I have changed my mind—it must be an orphanage that I will be running. Little children are so sad without their mummies and I will let them have a pussy each.' In this fantasy the lost kitten and the lost child have merged, and Jane sees her role in providing for them all the mothering that she herself lost when she was suddenly separated from her mother.

During this time Jane started looking after babies, especially one who, like herself, had no father. Jane proudly pointed out each of the baby's achievements, as if she were talking about her own child. In this she seemed fully identified with her mother, who had welcomed every new step in Jane's development with so much pride.

For a long time Jane's plans for the future had been entirely centred around the wish to become someone who could make lost animals or orphan children happy. Her mother then married a man who had lost his wife. He had a son who had been in an institution since his mother's death. When her mother hesitatingly approached Jane about her stepfather's son and his wish to have him at home, Jane insisted that he must not be left in the institution any longer and asked to be allowed to fetch him herself. It was decided that the little boy, who was five years old, should come home. Jane, aged 12 by then, took over the greatest part of his care, mothered him and, according to her mother, showed such real understanding of his needs and difficulties that she was able to help him adapt to family life, which he had hardly known before.

A year later, a former Nursery worker who visited the family reported: 'Jane is crazy about pets. In their small house at present live father, mother, the stepbrother, grandfather, uncle, aunt, and a boy cousin, but still they have room for a cat with two kittens, a dog and a puppy, and in the garden they have rabbits and chickens. Jane adores looking after them and loves puppies and chickens alike. She calls all these animals by name and wishes she could have more.

Reaction to mother's marriage

On the surface Jane seemed to adjust very well to the complete change from being her mother's only concern to having to share her not only with her husband but with the stepbrother who needed so much of her attention. During the same year, however, signs of withdrawal, dreaminess and a succession of fainting attacks made their appearance. Jane continued at first to be on friendly terms with her mother, and she made a good relationship with the stepfather. At the same time her teachers observed the symptoms mentioned above, which appeared mainly at school. It was not possible at the time to get insight into the conflicts aroused by the mother's marriage; and only recently, 12 years later, has Jane been able to give an account of some of her angry and disturbed feelings. She felt that her mother had let her down, not because she had married, but because she had changed in her behaviour towards her. She had become aggressive and short-tempered when Jane seemed to be interfering between her and her husband. In Jane's own words: 'It was as if I'd lost the mother I knew and had to get to know a new one; she was so different.' She felt that it was through the stepfather's kindness and understanding that she later regained her good relationship with her mother. The stepfather was fond of

Jane and said spontaneously: 'No man could wish for a kinder, better daughter; she makes us all happy.'

Jane's active moves towards independence

In following Jane's reaction to separation through puberty and adolescence, it becomes quite clear that she has actively arranged to be away from home more and more. At the same time, she is obviously happy to return there. Already from the age of 11 onward she went by train to a nearby town and spent all day at school, returning home in the evening. Soon after, she began to spend weekends and part of her holidays with friends. Throughout these years her interest in new people and places became an outstanding feature, and there are no signs that her increasing removal from the family circle is based on an angry wish to separate from her mother, as is often found in adolescents. On the contrary, according to both her mother's and her stepfather's accounts, her kindness and gaiety contribute greatly to the family's happiness. It appears, also, that the ever-growing difference between her own education and interests and those of her family does not form an obstacle. Jane, on the contrary, contributes by her new interests and does not hesitate to introduce her friends to the family.

After leaving school, Jane decided on a teacher's training college in London, which meant that she could live at home only during her holidays. At that time, when she was 18, she met questions about any anxious reaction to being away from her mother with astonishment and showed that she was totally unaware of the experience she had gone through when she was in her third year. She said that she had never felt anxious when away from home and developed plans to travel to foreign countries as soon as possible. These she carried out with much pleasure.

In her choice of career, Jane had moved away from the earlier fantasies of having to care for lost animals or children. What had remained was her wish to work with children. She felt that she was not the sort of person who could live in an institution, as would have been necessary if she had stuck to her earlier plan. She chose biology and physical education as her two subjects, because these had been her best subject in the last years at school. Her love of nature and the wish that children should be taught about animals and plants in a way that would make them really interested in rather than be bored by the lessons were topics that she discussed with enthusiasm. Her pleasure in her bodily skills and her talent for organization were directed towards planning games and competitions. At present she is in charge of all arrangements for outdoor activities of a large London grammar school, and she gets great satisfaction from planning both physical and intellectual activities outside the school, such as visits to sports events, museums, etc. She has won the cup in last year's yachting race of the seaside town where she lives and greatly enjoyed all the publicity and popularity among young people after this event.

Adult life in London

As an adult with a self-chosen satisfying career, Jane has organized her life to provide her with rich opportunities for both work and pleasure.

When I asked her to stay with me until she had found a flat, she did so with great pleasure, but her active search and her clear idea about what she was looking for made it possible for her to find what she wanted within a week. When asked what had determined her choice, she said: 'It has to be a place that is comfortable and attractive, where it is homey and I am independent at the same time.' This sentence characterizes her present relationship to her home and to me.

Further discussion of her choice of a flat has opened up the whole question of the role that I as her 'substitute mother' played in her development. Initially I had emerged from the number of nurses in the Hampstead Nursery to whom Jane had held on indiscriminately as the one she wanted in her mother's absence. Gradually she became closely attached to me. She first used me entirely as a substitute for her mother, to fulfill her needs as they made themselves felt. But I came to mean more than the person who provided her with what she really wanted from her mother. Later Jane was able to have a relationship with me as a person who was separate from her mother and to take and enjoy the new and different things she could get from me.

In Jane's personality, in her tastes and choice of career, it is possible to trace aspects of her identification with me. Jane has herself traced back some of these links and is conscious of them. In discussing her choice of flat, for instance, Jane said that as soon as she had seen the one that was furnished with period furniture, she no longer considered any one of the others. Thinking about her preference for this led her at first to my present house, which contains much antique furniture. She then remembered my room in the Hampstead Nursery, which had contained some of the same furniture and where Jane had spent much time. Jane also believes that her interest in foreign countries and especially foreign food is related to me who came from the Continent. Her earlier need for oral satisfaction is now largely satisfied through her pleasure in cooking and eating unusual dishes.

Conclusion

The knowledge of Jane's development and of her present personality is confined to those areas into which insight has been possible through direct observation by an analytically trained observer with whom she has maintained a warm and lasting relationship.

Insight into other aspects has not been possible. This is due partly to the fact that unconscious material was inaccessible, and partly to my gradually becoming aware that one large area of Jane's thinking and feeling cannot be approached, because it is blocked by far-reaching repression as well as by conscious reluctance to discuss this subject. It concerns all memories and feelings connected with her father, whom she knew up to the age of six and who visited her at the Nursery whenever he was on leave from the army. Jane maintains that she has no memory of him and has never mentioned a wish to contact him. She has formed a warm relationship with her stepfather and has at present a close relationship to a young man who shares her interests and whom she hopes to marry. In this she differs greatly from the many other illegitimate girls whom we have had the opportunity to study by direct observation or in analysis. It is so far impossible to say, however, whether her heterosexual relationship will be a well-adjusted one.

An assessment of Jane's present personality on the basis of the material available shows her to be a well-adjusted young woman who has been able to solve her conflicts without a far-reaching use of pathological mechanisms.

In her instinctual development, in her ego and superego, and in her object relationships, Jane functions on an adult level, with apparently little interference from inner conflicts. The only symptom that Jane occasionally shows in moments of tension is a brief and repeated sigh, which intersperses her speech. It is not impossible that analytic investigation would disclose the compression of a great deal of complex emotional material in this symptom.

The question poses itself which factors in the inner and outer conditions of her life have made it possible for this fatherless, homeless girl, who was severely traumatized through separation from her mother in the third year, to reach adulthood with as little apparent damage. Among the most important factors probably are the nature of Jane's personality, the developmental levels she had reached, and the good relationship with her mother before the separation. Although she regressed severely in both her libidinal and ego development, her innate capacities enabled her to make a forward move again within a comparatively short time.

It seems of great importance to me that at the time of separation Jane's development had been well advanced with regard to her object relationship and had undoubtedly reached the stage of object constancy. This enabled her to maintain the relationship with her mother in spite of the frequent interruptions during the first months of separation. This factor also made it possible for Jane to form a close and longlasting relationship with me after the first weeks of indiscriminate clinging. Although this relationship to me was at first characterized by features of need fulfillment and of the anaclitic stage, she was able to regain and later move forward to more advanced forms of object relationship.

The innate ego capacities—namely, her good intelligence and the unimpaired use of her capacity to verbalize—have played a large part in Jane's recovery. She emerged from the initial helplessly confused feeling about her mother's disappearances and reappearances by making use of the available clues that could lead to orientation in time and place. The trust in her mother, which had existed before the shock of being left, gradually reappeared, as the mother kept to the promises she made about her visits.

Furthermore, Jane's freedom to put her anger into words whenever her mother had disappointed her helped to reduce anxiety, especially as the mother responded freely with expressions of love and was able to tolerate Jane's anger without arousing undue guilt.

The interest in this long-term study lies in the fact that the observers who had seen the child during her traumatic experience in which she reacted with greatest distress had felt that this could not pass without interfering with Jane's further development and personality. Nevertheless, the observations of her development and the assessment of her present personality show that the trauma had neither stopped ongoing development nor left a disturbing mark on her adult life.

CHAPTER FOUR

Follow-up studies

I n the last chapter the Hampstead Nursery Follow-up Studies were illustrated by the case of Jane, studied over a period of 20 years. The necessary background material was already provided in a description of the work in the Hampstead War Nurseries (chapter 1) and of psychoanalytic material related to observations in early development (chapter 2).

The follow-up studies did not come to an end after 20 years. I remain a substitute mother for Jane in her adult role and am still in close contact with her after 48 years. But Jane was one of five children with whom I have also kept in close touch and whose adult development I am still able to follow closely. The early development of one of the children, Martin, has also been discussed in chapter 2. His great difficulty in loosening the tie to a mother who had maintained an infantile close physical relationship with continued and excessive oral gratification had seemed an insoluble problem. When his passivity and homosexual tendencies came to the fore, he returned to his analyst. His choice of career, which involves speaking, reading and a high level of literary appreciation as its basis, crystallised out during these years, alternating with deep despondency and self-devaluation, during which he worked as a labourer or dustman.

Guilt has played a large part in his life. It was conspicuous in adolescence, when he felt forced to loosen the infantile tie. His hostility and death wishes against his mother made the step away from her an extremely dangerous one, and only intensive analytic work made the move to another woman possible. He now has a nice home, a wife with whom he is happy and two daughters to whom he is a devoted father. In his thoughts and feelings for them, his determination to give them a stable home, his concern to avoid situations arousing anxiety for them (for example, when his older girl entered nursery school and later formal school), his memories played an important part. He has also read a great deal about children's upbringing, and he and his wife share their pleasure in the girls.

Bob's early development is briefly discussed in the first chapter. When he was three yeas old, his father was simply the image of a person whom he could love and admire and show off proudly to other people. At three-and-a-half years, Bobbie used his father image as a representation of his own destructive wishes; at four years his father became the embodiment of everything that was big, beautiful, strong and good. At four and a half the fantasy-father definitely took over the role of the boy's conscience, which had developed in the meantime. It was then and has remained an over-severe conscience.

Bob became attached to his substitute mother in a demanding way and made slow progress. His mother visited irregularly, bringing a variety of men with her. Life with her from seven-and-a-half years did not lead to a good relationship with her. He left to join the Army at 16. He then studied to become an accountant and went to Australia. He has done a great deal to make up for his poor education, studying history. He became severely obese and depressed and had relations with neither men or women. He was compelled to carry sugar lumps with him. When treatment was arranged for him, he broke it off after three sessions.

It is of interest that Martin, as well as twins for whom I also became a substitute mother, also showed extremes of idealization and excessively aggressive and destructive features about a figure who did not exist in reality—where the absence of a constant relationship to a father or father substitute prevented reality testing, and identification with the real person onto whom love, hate and consequent fear could be projected.

The twins themselves have been discussed in Dorothy Burlingham's (1952) book on the subject and were known as Jessy and Bessy. Here, I will add only a few words about them. Reasons of confidentiality preclude further extended discussion.

Guilt has played a large part in the lives of both of them. In Jessy's case guilt led to self-punishment from time to time and is still a problem to her, although she can come and show a conscious awareness of the reasons for her need to destroy her happiness. Her ambivalence against her mother and the attendant and recurrent guilt forces her to relive her mother's life in fantasy. This occurs especially at times when her real life is happy. She can admit this only with great difficulty. When she is conscious of having achieved what she has been longing for, the urge to destroy her happiness overtakes her. Her mother's life preoccupies her in every detail.

Recently she said guiltily: 'Do you realize that I have literally got everything I have always been hoping for?—A profession I like and am successful in, the house of my dreams, within easy reach of Hampstead, two children, a boy and a girl, and a husband who has been kind to me for ten years, although I know that I have been very unkind to him for much of the time. He has even become brighter and more successful, so I don't have to be ashamed of him any more. Perhaps I have too much.'

Her twin, Bessy, is not happily married. They made their choice of partners, similar in each case, on the basis of identi-

fication, choosing husbands who had been deprived in childhood and were depressed. Jessy's and Bessy's narcissism
makes them unable to love and care for their husbands
without resentment. Jessy's feelings are characterized in the
answer she gave her husband when he asked why she had not
prepared any Sunday lunch. 'I'm not hungry', she said.

PART TWO

Simultaneous analysis

CHAPTER FIVE

Simultaneous analysis
of parent and child

I n certain cases, treatment of the child does not proceed
satisfactorily without simultaneous treatment of one or
both parents. This fact has been recognized by child
analysts for many years and has led to the development of
various techniques to deal with the problem. In child guidance practice, regular contact with one or both parents is
maintained by a staff member, while the child's treatment is
carried out by the psychiatrist or therapist in charge. The
nature of the work done with parents ranges from discussing
practical problems arising from the child's treatment to psychotherapeutic intervention, which aims at dealing with the

A version of this paper appeared in I. Glenn (ed.), *Child Analysis
and Therapy* (New York/London: Jason Aronson, 1978), pp. 473–491.

The author wishes to express her thanks to Dorothy Burlingham,
who was the originator of the Hampstead Study and whose encouragement and advice helped her throughout, and to Dr Liselotte Frankl for
the help she has given her.

parents' own disturbance. A great deal of literature on the various approaches within child guidance work has accumulated. However, a review of this literature is beyond the scope of the present discussion, which is confined to simultaneous psychoanalytic treatment of parent and child. The total number of simultaneous analysis cases that have been studied is small. This is not because of a lack of interest or awareness of the need for simultaneous analyses but is essentially due to problems of availability of psychoanalysis in clinic settings, financial reasons and the difficulties involved in publishing material referring to patients in private practice. Assessment of work carried out by simultaneous analysis is therefore confined to the small number of cases published, and to some unpublished cases that form part of the 'Study on Simultaneous Analysis' carried out at the Hampstead Child Therapy Clinic, London.

Therapeutic aims

One aim of simultaneous analysis has been to provide psychoanalytic treatment for parents and children who have been unresponsive to more superficial forms of treatment. In addition, simultaneous analysis attempts to provide the chance of successful treatment for children whose progress in analysis had been interfered with by the intensity and nature of his parent's pathology. In Anna Freud's words (1960a): 'Where the neurotic symptom, the conflict or the regression of a child is anchored not only in the young patient's own personality but held in place further by powerful emotional forces in the parent to whom the child is tied, the therapeutic action of analysis may well be slowed up or, in extreme cases, made impossible' (p. 379). If simultaneous treatment of the parent takes place: 'The interpretations to the child [may] become effective, or . . . regressive libidinal

positions given up in direct relation to the parent's relinquishing either a fixed pathological position of her own, or in
other cases, relinquishing a pathological hold on the child' (p.
379).

Simultaneous analysis can also provide treatment for
children whose parents feel disturbed by one or more aspects
of treatment, or by changes in the child resulting from it.

> Rachel's mother found it intolerable to feel her little girl's
> growing attachment to her analyst. She felt intense jeal-
> ousy and interfered with the child's treatment by cancell-
> ing sessions, coming late and ridiculing the analyst.
>
> Rachel's mother reacted to changes in her child. When
> Rachel began to become active and aggressive as a result
> of treatment, instead of remaining passive and inhibited,
> her mother reacted with anger. She attempted to make her
> daughter submissive again, even though she realized
> Rachel was improving at her school work and in her rela-
> tionships with other children.

In addition, parents are often fearful their children will
divulge family secrets to the analyst. A full description of
this situation and its destructive effect on the child's treatment was given by Dorothy Burlingham (1935b) and has
been confirmed in cases reported by other analysts. Gradual
changes in the parent's feelings, fantasies, and conflicts concerning their child and their growing insight generally leads
to an awareness of the nature of their interference with the
child's ongoing development. Also, parents frequently
become aware of the aspects of treatment that arouse their
anxiety, jealousy or other conflicting feelings. Such feelings
frequently compel them to interfere with or even termi-
nate their child's treatment.

Research aims

Clarification of developmental problems

The use of simultaneous analysis aims at clarifying a wide variety of developmental problems. The coordination of available material from concurrent analyses provides access to the unconscious meaning and motivation of parent–child interactions. This is needed for a fuller understanding of material from direct observation of manifest behaviour between parent and child. Simultaneous analysis attempts to answer questions about the pathogenic effect of a parent's pathology on the child from birth, and throughout subsequent phases of development. Evidence is sought for the correctness or incorrectness of certain assumptions and is looked for in the material of both patients.

Understanding the interaction between parents and their children is of the highest importance during the period when the foundations of the personality are laid and the bases for mental illness are established. It continues to remain important as the child grows. As a child moves forward on the developmental scale, each step demands giving up former positions and gains, not only from the child, but from the parent too. It is only in the most healthy and normal cases that both parent and child wholly welcome progressive moves and enjoy the child's increasing maturity and gradually increasing independence. More often, one or the other partner lags behind. The child is unable to free himself from fixations, or the parent clings to attitudes of protectiveness and mothering that are no longer justified. In the worst cases, mother and child join forces in a regressive move. Such interlocking becomes particularly fateful at the onset of puberty. The simultaneous analyses of mothers and their adolescent children allow us to study the various ways in which individual adolescents strive to free themselves from infantile ties to their parents. While we receive no more than a dim impression of the parent's responses in cases where the adolescent alone is in treatment, simultaneous analysis enables us to trace each party's contribution to the success or failure of this developmental task.

Links between the parent's and child's pathologies

Simultaneous analysis aims at obtaining a clearer understanding of the relation between the parent's disturbance and the child's abnormal development. This is done by comparing details of their libidinal and aggressive feelings, fantasies and anxieties, and the nature of the defense mechanisms used by both parent and child. In this way, interferences with the child's progress are clarified.

Means of communication between parent and child

The pathways of unconscious communication through which various elements of the parent's pathology reach the child and affect it at various developmental stages were traced. Differentiation between pre-verbal, nonverbal and verbal communication and between fantasy expressed in action or contained in the parent's mind and the child's responses to the various ways communication reached him was established with considerable clarity in some areas but remained diffuse in others.

Dorothy Burlingham (Burlingham, Goldberger & Lussier, 1955) clearly showed that in cases where a mother's fantasies lead to action and her child was used to satisfy her own libidinal or aggressive needs, analysis was not able to free the child from the effect of his mother's interference. Had the mother's fantasies remained within her thoughts and feelings or had they been expressed verbally, the outcome would have been different. In the case of Bobby, aged three, analysis was able to free him from the effect of his mother's verbal communications. Although his fantasies had originated in his mother's unconscious, they had become Bobby's.

They had undergone his elaborations and had led to defenses. Therefore they could be dealt with analytically.

Clarification of concepts

Simultaneous analysis also aims at clarifying certain concepts that have been widely accepted and made use of in the past 40 years. We are particularly interested in clarifying the tendency to make mothers responsible for a wide variety of childhood disturbances. This tendency has led to many pronouncements and to the use of global terms that are in need of differentiation. The great variety and subtlety of the ways in which various aspects of the mother's personality affect her child at different stages of development seemed in danger of oversimplification. Through simultaneous analysis, this danger has been counteracted as the complicated network of interaction can be traced. One of the concepts that tends to obscure deeper understanding is the much-used term *the rejecting mother*. The multiplicity of factors included in this term was demonstrated by Anna Freud (1955). All subsequent simultaneous analyses of mothers and children have given evidence of the complicated interplay of factors that become blurred when this concept is used. The term *overprotective mother,* though indicating one aspect visible to the observer, equally obscures the network of mutual responses that needs to be understood through analytic insight.

Methods used in studies of simultaneous analyses

A variety of methods were used by different analysts in their research work.

The same analyst treating both mother and child

In her study of children suffering from ulcerative colitis, Melitta Sperling (1946) treated both mother and child herself in separate sessions. She felt it was preferable that the child did not know his mother was in treatment. This practice seems unwise, as it may interfere with the analyst's objective and neutral attitude towards both patients. Keeping secrets may also destroy the child's faith in his analyst's integrity. The child may suspect the therapist is treating his mother on the sly. Joyce McDougall (Lebovici & McDougall, 1969) also treated both mother and son. However, the mother became her patient only after the boy had terminated his analysis and had gone to boarding school in another country.

Different analysts treating mother and child

In the research project on simultaneous analysis carried out at the Hampstead Child-Therapy Clinic, London, all analyses of parents and children were carried out by two different analysts to reduce interference with normal analytic work to a minimum.

To study the material of both patients, a third analyst acted as coordinator. Analysts reported their material weekly to this coordinator. This method was introduced into the Hampstead Study by Dorothy Burlingham (Burlingham et al., 1955) and was followed by the coordinators of all subsequent cases with one exception. Kata Levy (1960) analysed a mother and also acted as coordinator in a case involving an adolescent girl.

In most cases, the analysts of parent and child did not communicate with each other, and the coordinator did not disclose material from the other patient to the reporting analyst. It was felt that knowledge of the child's or parent's analysis might interfere with the analytic work. Acting as coordinator in two studies, Ilse Hellman (Hellman, Friedmann & Shepheard, 1960; Hellman, de Monchaux & Ludowyk-Gyomroi, 1961) used different methods for each. One study was carried out on the same lines as those generally adopted for the Hampstead Clinic Research. The patients' material was not communicated to the respective analysts. In the second study, the coordinator informed both analysts of the material, or they were present while reports were given to the coordinator. Each analyst was free to discuss details of the material of both patients as it emerged. The purpose of this comparison of methods was an attempt to gain some insight into the helpful and detrimental aspects of knowledge of the parent's or child's material on each analyst's handling of his case.

At the conclusion of this study, both analysts felt their technique had not been different, in spite of knowing the other patient's material. Interpretations were based only on their own patient's material and its transference implications. However, it became clear that the understanding of certain aspects of the child's material and increased certainty concerning differentiation between the child's fantasies and factual information were reached through knowledge of the mother's material. This referred especially to facts concerning the mother's sexual stimulation of her child. The child alluded to it in play and in symbolic form, but the fact that this was an ongoing experience had never been stated by the child.

In other cases as well, sexual experiences were left out by the child or referred to only in veiled form. In these cases, analysts were not informed of the parent's material, and the children did not refer to parental seductions as real experiences. This did not allow clear differentiation between reality and fantasy.

Main findings concerning the pathogenic effect of the parent on the child

Detailed study of the psychoanalytic material of parents and children in concurrent analyses has clearly shown that simple conclusions about the effect of parental psychopathology on children are misleading. That a multiplicity of factors is involved has been impressively shown. Guidelines leading to a clarification of understanding these pathogenic effects have emerged from all cases and have thrown light on the nature and degree of interference different elements of the parent's personality have on the child.

Interference with child's development

Approached from the developmental point of view, we can assess favourable and unfavourable conditions to which the child is exposed at each stage. A mother's symptom may contain features that provide her child with age-adequate experience on one level yet hinder normal progress on the next.

An example of this is found in mothers who experience intense anxiety when their child is not close to them physically. They either unconsciously feel the child as part of themselves or need close contact to counteract hostility and guilt. These mothers' urge to hold and handle their child provides the young baby with the age-adequate experience of closeness to her. However, in the course of the first year, and increasingly from then on, this same baby experiences his mother's need for closeness more and more as an obstacle to the new developmental steps he is ready to take. The baby's need to move further from her, to explore his surroundings through increasing motor control and to experience new objects, activities and people can meet with his mother's continued attempts to extend the previous phase, when the child's need for closeness gave her the satisfaction she needed to keep her anxiety at a bearable level.

Mrs A frequently spoke of the 'terrible experience' it was for her when her son became physically independent and began to sit up and walk. She was compelled to push him back into the lying position and to prevent him from walking. His spontaneous change of position made her feel helpless and angry. His attempts to walk brought the feeling he was 'walking away' from her, and rejecting her. Eric therefore had difficulty progressing past the practicing subphase of separation–individuation. [Mahler, Pine & Bergman, 1975]

In these situations, conflicts are produced in the child between his active wishes, which may lead him to aggressive attempts to free himself from his mother's interference, and passive submission to her demands and prohibitions. Quick alternation of intense gratification and frustration experienced through the mother lays the foundation for a sado-masochistic relationship with her, with alternation of love, hate and guilt as the pattern of their mutual interaction. Separation–individuation cannot take place normally. Such relationships are well known from direct observation of mothers and babies. However, the unconscious reasons different mothers need to use their children to deal with their own anxiety can only become known through their analysis. The child's reactions and his fears and fantasies in response to the use his mother made of him can only be gained from subsequent analysis through reconstruction and through his play and verbal communications, once he has reached the age when they become analysable.

The situation described above was found in four cases studied at the Hampstead Child Therapy Clinic. In each case, the mother's ambivalence was the main reason for her need to keep the child close and well protected. These mothers were all guilty about a previous abortion and had wished to abort the child they subsequently were constantly concerned with.

In contrast to mothers compelled to keep their babies close to them, other cases were studied where mothers were unable to tolerate their babies' physical closeness and had deprived them of this experience. Both types of disturbance belong to a category of mothers referred to by Anna Freud (1960a). She points out that their illness interfered with their capacity for *effective mothering*. Without age-adequate need satisfaction, children of such mothers develop a wide range of disturbances. The following material from the analysis of Mrs Z (Hellman, Schnurmann & Todes, 1970) can serve as illustration.

Mrs Z could not look at or hold her baby with pleasure. Feeling Rachel suck her nipples was an ordeal. All Mrs Z 's attempts to feed her baby were unsuccessful. She felt the baby was 'sucking her dry' but simultaneously had fantasies she was starving Rachel. Therefore Mrs Z was compelled to overfeed her daughter, causing her to be sick frequently. Mrs Z 's mother had been unable to feed her, and this played an important part in this mother's fantasies about her own emptiness. Deprived of adequate mothering and feeding in this early phase, the baby was exposed to painful experiences resulting from her mother's guilt. The fear of starving her child led this mother to overfeed her, and this led to the child's digestive troubles. The foundation was laid for Rachel's oral fixation. It played a central part in the disturbance for which she was referred for analysis at the age of four. Rachel's problems included excessive eating alternating with sickness, obesity and overdependence on her mother, to whom she was ambivalently attached.

Obesity: a symptom in mother and child

Both mother and daughter were addicted to food, and both were obese. It became clear from the mother's material that she was repeating with her daughter what she felt she had been made to experience by her own mother. She thought of her mother as a 'food giver, not a love giver.' Also, she felt her mother was unable to love a female child. In her analysis, Rachel's mother discovered with great guilt that she, too, was a 'food giver, not a love giver' and that she could not love Rachel, because she was a girl. She was compelled to make Rachel experience what she had. Unable to love her daughter, she used food as a substitute. In Rachel's analysis, it became possible to clarify the link between her eating compulsion and her use of food as a substitute for mother's love. This was one important aspect of her symptom of overeating.

In the mother's fantasies, food not only represented a substitute for love. It was also a hostile weapon that she could use to harm the child, making her sick, fat and ugly. It had the twofold function of punishing the child and ultimately punishing herself.

In Rachel's material, a clear division was seen between good, comforting food, standing for the love substitute, and bad, sick-making and fattening food, representing the mother's hate. Rachel had to submit to eating 'bad food' to retain her mother's approval, and to punish herself for hating her. A similar incapacity to handle and feed infants was found in other mothers in the Hampstead study. Eric's mother had unsuccessfully tried to abort him. When he was born, she felt she could not touch and hold him. However, she could not allow anyone else to look after him for any length of time because she felt guilty and jealous, particularly when her husband tried to comfort Eric.

Mother's fear of poisoning the child— child's fear of being poisoned

Mrs A's guilt about her attempted abortion and her continued death wishes were expressed in constant fears of poisoning her child with bad food. This persisted throughout his childhood, and played a central part in his life when he was referred for treatment at age eleven. Eric responded to his mother's fear of poisoning him by experiencing intense fears of being poisoned by her and by feeling sick. He gradually developed revenge fantasies and would punish her by exaggerated sickness and becoming unable to attend school.

He forced his mother to stay home with him and to buy luxury food that she could not afford.

In all the cases in which mothers experienced feelings of hostility and guilt in relation to their babies from birth, interference with feeding had led to symptom formation centring on food and to a relationship in which ambivalence and distrust led to a prolonged dependence on the mother.

Abnormal concern with their children's digestion and defecation was found in all mothers whose anxieties about feeding were essentially based on their ambivalence. They constantly needed to ascertain that their death wishes did not come true by either starving the child or giving him bad food. Their attitudes towards cleanliness varied according to their own developments in the anal phase. In two cases, behaviour based on unusually great undefended satisfaction in their children's defecation and urination was found.

Claudia's mother had been a bedwetter throughout her childhood and well into adolescence. She had been unable to train Claudia and showed no concern about her daughter's continued wetting. She derived pleasure from having the child in bed with her even though she was wet. Her behaviour made it plain to Claudia that her mother experienced sympathy with her when others in the household insisted on training her. Claudia's bed-wetting, which persisted into late adolescence, was partly a response to her mother's wish that Claudia would be just as she was as a child—stupid and infantile. Claudia's analysis showed her compliance with her mother's fantasy formed only part of the reason for her symptom. Claudia's own sexual anxieties and an early seduction by an uncle were responsible for Claudia's fantasy that she had nothing inside her to hold in the flow of urine. This long-lasting symptom led to intense experiences of shame and added to her self-devaluation, which also resulted from her pseudo-stupidity.

Bobby's mother also achieved satisfaction through participating in the process of her child's elimination. Toilet training had led to a complicated ritual between him and his mother. This was described in detail by Dorothy Burlingham

(Burlingham, Goldberger, & Lussier, 1955). Bobby's fears of emptiness if he let his faeces go and fears of fullness if he held them in alternated. His mother had had similar fears in her own childhood and had insisted on keeping her mother's attention during defecation. The analysis clearly showed Bobby's own fantasies were responsible for the conflict he experienced at the moment of defecation. However, his mother's attitude, combined with her own fantasies about her body content, united them in the daily ritual.

Cases in which the mother's reaction formation led to intense disgust and to an insistence on early cleanliness were studied by Melitta Sperling (1946). She analysed mothers and children suffering from ulcerative colitis and found that one important factor in this illness was that it gave the mothers 'legitimate' gratification of their repressed anal-erotic and anal-sadistic needs. The children responded with early intense reaction formation and showed disgust at an unusually early age. However, their symptom gave both mother and child gratification through its messiness. Both joined in conscious disgust and unconscious gratification.

Premature sexual stimulation

Children used by their mothers from babyhood onwards as partners in sexual games display the effects of serious interference with all important aspects of normal development. Mrs A used Eric to relive the sexual experiences she had with her younger brother throughout her childhood. She had played the male role in these games and stimulated her brother and penetrated his mouth with her tongue. She began this practice with Eric when he was a baby and discontinued it when he was 12 years old, after they had both been in analysis for over a year. Eric's symptom of vomiting was found to be related to these experiences, as well as to his fantasy of being poisoned, which he shared with his mother. The most damaging elements of his mother's stimulation arose from his states of excitation throughout the pre-genital and phallic stages. Eric was forced into passivity during this stimulation. His latency development was hindered as a consequence. The pathological aspects of his pre-oedipal and oedipal relationship with his mother, who was felt to be an overwhelming, threatening figure, made his entry into puberty very difficult. He experienced the main developmental problems of adolescence in a highly pathological way.

Another mother initiated premature sexual stimulation in her baby's first year and continued until she had been in analysis for a considerable time. Mrs Z. was compulsively concerned with her baby's masturbation. According to her, her daughter had masturbated intensely from the age of nine months. It was clear Mrs Z. initiated her baby's first genital explorations, while she had watched intently and with mounting excitement. Mrs Z. described reaching an orgasm-like experience and expected to see her child experience an orgasm too. Analysis clarified the link between the mother's own compulsive masturbation in childhood and the reenactment with Rachel. Mrs Z. had denied being a girl, had been envious of her brother and had played sexual games with him. Her disappointment that Rachel was a girl formed part of the hostility she experienced against her daughter. In the sexual play, Rachel partly represented Mrs Z.'s brother. This denied Rachel was a girl. The mother played the male role in the fantasy. Rachel's response to her mother's persistent stimulation was enacted in her treatment sessions and was brought into the transference through exhibitionistic masturbation and excitation.

In these cases, as well as in the study of Bobby and his mother by Dorothy Burlingham (Burlingham, Goldberger & Lussier, 1955), and Claudia and her mother by Ilse Hellman (Hellman, de Monchaux & Ludowyk-Gyomroi, 1961), the mothers' use of their children for sexual excitation and satisfaction led to long-lasting disturbances. In those cases where the child's treatment extended into puberty and adolescence, it became especially clear how the premature stimulation by the mother and the continued use of the children for sexual satisfaction had affected all important areas of their personalities.

The main conflicts of adolescence (A. Freud, 1958) were intensified, and the development towards a separate identity was difficult to attain even with long analyses. Libidinal and aggressive impulses were excessively heightened in response to the mother's changing behaviour and the affective states accompanying it. The degree of anxiety arising from these experiences made the use of pathological defenses necessary. Sublimations were found to be severely disrupted through the libidinization and aggressivization of a variety of activities. Frustration tolerance was very poor, and superego development was distorted as a result of the child's viewing the mother as a seductive, guilty partner who was also extremely threatening. Severe interference with normal oedipal development was found in all the cases studied. This was especially marked where the mothers used their children for sexual satisfaction from an early age. The children's approach to their fathers and the fathers' relationship to their children were disturbed by the mother's denigration of the father and her jealousy whenever the child showed signs of enjoying the father's company.

Eric's mother created a distorted picture of his father. She constantly ridiculed her husband's lack of education and emphasized he had lost a thumb and was therefore clumsy. This denigration of the father and her attempts to prevent a good relationship between him and the boy extended throughout Eric's childhood. Only after long analysis was he able to feel free enough to admit his love and admiration for his father. He was then able to see his father as the man he really was and became able to identify and enjoy common interests with him.

Parents who are as disturbed as those included in the study of simultaneous analyses do not have marital relationships that allow their children to develop under conditions favourable for establishing a normal oedipal phase.

Marjorie Sprince (1962) described the case of Debby, whose father's close relationship to her was distorted by his pathology. His disturbance made him deeply concerned about her digestion. Both parents were closely involved with each other's and Debbie's hypochondriacal fantasies about food and digestive illness. Forward moves in Debbie's development were shortlived, and regression to oral and anal fixation points occurred again and again as these fixations were anchored in both the maternal and the paternal relationship.

Divorce and illegitimacy were the cause of abnormal oedipal development in the other cases. Claudia's mother was promiscuous and unable to tell the child who her father was. Claudia maintained a close pre-oedipal attachment to her mother. In adolescence, her search for her fantasy father was acted out. Claudia became promiscuous as her mother had been, not merely due to identification, but as a result of other inner conflicts as well.

There had been severe interference with George's oedipal development. George's mother left the family after several extramarital relationships and abortions. The simultaneous treatment of seven-and-a-half-year-old George and his father was coordinated by Liselotte Frankl (1965). His father refused to allow a woman to join the household to look after George and his younger brother. This was based on his fantasy of wanting to be both a mother and father to his children. In his attempts to be close to George, he essentially made him a partner in his own depression and did not succeed in giving the child necessary care because of his ambivalence. The boy's fantasies evoked intense fears of his mother as a dangerous, destructive woman, and his aggressive wishes against her dominated his thoughts. Simultaneously, homosexual fears were expressed in the material of both father and son. Scenes of aggressive attacks took place, which led to George's fantasies of taking up a woman's role with his father. Forward moves towards heterosexuality and the sublimations characteristic of latency emerged only slowly after both father and son had been in treatment for several years.

The child is used to fulfill mother's ambition

Parents' fantasies of achieving success which remain unfulfilled were found to govern their relationship to their child as he grew older, particularly when he reached school age. In two cases, the first signs of this attitude had become manifest by the onset of speech development.

Eric's and Rachel's mothers were concerned with their children's speech. They showed marked competitiveness with the achievements of other children of the same age and spent a great deal of time talking and reading to their children. This had marked favourable results, and the children responded well to the amount of interest shown to them by their mothers. However, these mothers also put pressure on their children and expressed anger and ridicule when their fantasies of outstanding success did not come true. These aspects by far outweighed the favourable effects and created feelings of anxiety and hostility in the children. Pleasure and pride in their own achievements were interfered with, and self-esteem became uneven because of the extreme changes in their mother's responses to them.

For Eric's and Rachel's mothers, speaking well had been important in their childhoods. This related to intense competition with older brothers and also meant they might fulfill a wish to reach higher cultural and special levels than the male members of their families. For Eric's mother, who competed with her husband in every possible way, this had an important meaning. Eric was felt to be a part of his mother, and his speech had to be like hers. This meant he should not speak like his father, who had a working-class accent. Eric became able to speak well, but his verbal attacks against his mother alternated with a growing reluctance to talk to her at all. He found he could take revenge against her by attacking her with his great verbal skill and by withholding communication. In addition, speaking badly, which meant being like his father, was used as a weapon against her.

Mrs Z's use of Rachel to fulfill her own intellectual ambitions became marked in the later stages of her analysis. She deprived her child of any feeling that her school successes gave her pleasure, because Mrs Z was compelled to point out the negative aspects of Rachel's work. She also criticized the positive aspects, which were never felt to be good enough.

The child represents the damaged aspect of the mother

In the analyses of David and his mother (Burlingham, Schnurmann & Lantos, 1958), much of the mother's approach to her son was based on the unconscious identification of him with aspects of herself she felt were abnormal and damaged. Analysis further showed she saw David as she imagined her own mother had seen her. She was constantly worried he was lonely and unhappy at school. His unusually intense fantasy life disturbed her. He was pale and thin and spoke so faintly that the teacher could not hear him. This description exactly fitted the mother when she was a child. She too had been pale, thin and anxious, spoke in a faint voice and felt she was no good.

It appeared that David felt and behaved as his mother expected him to. He developed an identification not only with his mother, but with her image of him, which she conveyed in words and actions. Their communications by drawings and in fantasies about animals showed an unusually close understanding of one another. Her constant doubt of David's abilities prevented him from enjoying and fully developing them. She could never accept the reality of his successes and found it difficult to enjoy his growing independence.

Pseudo-stupidity:
a symptom found in mother and daughter

Claudia's mother's unconscious need to force her child into her own childhood role was clear. This led to the impression they shared a symptom. While certain symptoms appear to be the same in mother and child, their different structures become apparent through analytic work. It becomes possible to differentiate between those elements of each patient's conflicts that led to symptom formation, and those mechanisms that interact and contribute to the need to maintain the symptom. Both mother and daughter had the symptom of pseudo-stupidity. It was clear each needed the denial and confusion in her own mind for defensive purposes. However, it was also possible to trace the mother's unconscious need to make her daughter relive her own role of the stupid child.

The mother's constant anxiety throughout childhood led her to play the role of the stupid girl in her family. This was the 'safe role' in relation to her frightening mother and two older sisters. Her confusion, largely expressed in the use of nonsense words, protected her from expressing her hostility and envy and against the dangers that might have resulted from it. The mother's symptom resulted from her confusion between the sexes, and from her displacement onto the intellectual field of a conviction that she was damaged. Her blatant misuse of words and lack of knowledge of simple facts was used to display this damage, not only defensively, but to arouse interest and sympathy. Exhibiting her stupidity, misery, or poverty enabled her to receive kindness and sympathy from both her parents. The far-reaching use of the mechanism of denial was found to have a serious pathogenic effect.

Claudia's developing capacity to show curiosity made it possible to link her confusion and 'stupidity' to her unknown father. The urgency of Claudia's curiosity, her fear of asking and her distrust of what she was told showed the intensity of her conflict. It had a far-reaching inhibiting effect on her capacity to think and learn. The part her mother's disturbance played in this symptom was gradually clarified. This was the first and clearest link found in Claudia's far-reaching denial of reality and her need to embellish and blur the facts of her own life. Claudia's analysis was very successful in this area. Her later school achievements, as well as her work attainments shown in a follow-up 20 years later, showed that analysis had been able to free her from 'stupidity.' It had originated in her mother's unconscious wish to keep her daughter dependent and closely linked to her through the shared symptom. The mother's confused thinking was also much improved through her treatment, and she became able to enjoy Claudia's intellectual achievements. Consciously, mothers aim to shield their children from experiencing the miseries of their own childhood. However, analysis shows their deep-rooted need to make their children repeat the fate of the devalued child they had felt themselves to be.

The damaging influence of a mother's rigid reaction formations is well known. It has a detrimental effect on the child, particularly in the anal phase, when cleanliness training becomes important. Two other defense mechanisms and their damaging effects have become especially clear in these studies.

Effects of defense mechanisms:
the mother's denial of reality

If a mother's acceptance of external reality is disturbed, frequently these same areas remain unavailable to her child. Magical thinking, and the omnipotent denial the mother uses to avoid the intolerable facts of external and internal reality, are introjected by her child. He then operates with her mechanisms in these same areas, in the service of his own defenses. The child's attempts at reality testing are experienced by both mother and child as a danger. To the mother, the danger arises from the fear she will be forced to face the intolerable facts of reality through her child. To the child, reality testing and the acceptance of facts that are not in accordance with his mother's distorted picture brings the threat of loss of love and his mother's hostility, guilt and depression.

Effects of defense mechanisms:
the mother's projections

Some mothers make extensive use of their children as objects of projection. Coleman, Kris and Provence (1953) formulated that for such mothers, 'the child has not become an individual; he remains a projective screen' (p. 27). These mothers cannot react to their children's needs and impulses on the basis of a perception of their children's internal situation. Instead, they respond in line with their own projections. The manifestations and changing needs of the child call up a succession of different infantile conflicts in the mother. As these become pre-conscious, they bring manifestations of the mother's own early anxieties, fantasies and defenses. The child successively stands for these and for different early, conflicting objects in the mother's past. The persistent exposure to his mother's changing projections is severely damaging to a growing child. It interferes with establishing separateness from his mother and differentiating between his own impulses and anxieties and hers.

Therapeutic results

All mothers had come into treatment only after their children's analysts had indicated that their participation in the children's disturbance presented a serious obstacle to therapeutic success. Only Mr N had been in treatment previously. He had felt the need for help with his depression. None of the mothers had sought analysis to change or to gain insight into her own and her child's disturbance. In most of these mothers, guilt about their children's conditions led them to feel they must accept treatment. The therapeutic alliance was characterized by this situation and also by the fact that treatment was free. Therapeutic results were clearly influenced by these factors. Although insight was gained and favourable changes occurred, the parents, who did not seek analysis for their own sakes, tended to develop a limited therapeutic alliance and achieved limited therapeutic goals. These parents' withdrawal from treatment indicated that their desire for treatment was based largely on guilt concerning their children's disturbance.

Conclusions

Further studies are needed. Ideally these should arise from analytic work with young women who come to or are in analysis with an awareness of their need for it. Under these circumstances, the child subsequently taken into treatment would have a better chance to benefit from changes in his mother and from insight she would gain through treatment. Ideally, preventive work should be done by promoting treatment for pregnant women who feel ambivalent about motherhood. Any analysis of a mother carried out after her child has become disturbed and has reached the age when he is analysable cannot deal with the damage done to the baby during his first year. This has been demonstrated by cases in which the very capacity for mothering was interfered with, and in cases in which premature sexual stimulation took place.

This survey contains the main findings that emerged from the available material. The examples were chosen to illustrate what seemed to be the most typical effects of parents' pathology on their children. A large amount of material from both the parent's and the child's analysis seems to contain further aspects of more subtle pathological interactions. However, none of the authors found indications in the material clear enough to draw definite conclusions. Several coordinators expressed the wish that further research be carried out under planned conditions. Cases could then be chosen according to the pathology presented by either parent or child, or according to the type of developmental problem manifested by the child. Alternatively, attention could be focussed primarily on preventive work; for this, young children would be selected as they reach the age of analysability.

The present material has clarified areas in which treatment of a child without simultaneous treatment of the parent would either have failed or produced at most very limited therapeutic results. This study has also contributed to an awareness that inadequate need fulfilment in a child's earliest phases can lead to irreversible damage. In addition, the material contains ample proof of the severe pathogenic effect of premature sexual stimulation (see Greenacre, 1952).

CHAPTER SIX

Simultaneous analysis of mother and child

with Oscar Friedmann
and Elizabeth Shepheard

I n chapter 5 a general account was given of the research
project entitled 'Simultaneous Analysis of Parent and
Child' and how it came into being, illustrating various
aspects of its work with brief clinical vignettes. We now want
to take one of the child–parent couples mentioned there—
namely, Mrs A and Eric—and submit their concurrent analyses to more detailed study.

Based on a paper read at the Scientific Meeting of the Dutch Psycho-
Analytical Society, Amsterdam, on 23 October 1959, and at the British
Psycho-Analytical Society, London, on 2 December 1959. It was originally published in the *Psychoanalytic Study of the Child*, (1960)
15:359–377. The study was financed by the Psychoanalytic Research
and Development Fund Inc., New York.

Background data

When Mrs A and Eric first came to the Hampstead Clinic, the staff members recognized in them many of the well-known traits of mother-and-son couples who consult paediatric outpatient clinics before they finally reach child guidance. Winnicott (1948) has described such couples in his paper, 'Reparation in respect of the mother's organised defense.' He speaks of the narrow demarcation line that exists between a mother's normal hypochondriacal fears for her child and her pathological hypochondriasis, which extends to the child's body. He mentions a boy who came to his outpatient clinic alone, saying: 'Please Doctor, my Mum complains of pains in my tummy.'

In Eric's case there was a little doubt about the demarcation line. One was struck at once by the intensity of the mother's hypochondriacal fears concerning her boy; and the boy was already beyond bringing his mother's complaint of his fears and pains. It was clear that his fears of illness were already his own, as well as his mother's. He seemed aware of the internalization that had taken place, when early in his treatment he said to his therapist, referring to his digestion: 'Once, only Mum used to worry, now it's me.'

The concurrent analyses brought simultaneous experiences of anxiety about their health and bodily pains to light. This was one of the main areas of interaction. The other, closely related to it, concerned the interplay of the unconscious meaning that feeding and eating had in the relation of mother and son. Both of these led to the boy's inability to separate from his mother and consequently to his refusal to go to school. He had never left her before he went to the hospital for tonsillectomy at the age of three years. His panic at the separation was such that he was returned to his mother after one day. The operation was finally carried out at the age of five, when he submitted to it passively.

If Eric had developed only somatic symptoms, they would probably not have come for child guidance but continued to make the rounds of paediatric outpatient departments of famous hospitals. But suddenly, at the age of 11, Eric became unable to attend school. He had been a successful pupil and had recently won a grammar school place without difficulty; he had an I.Q. of 132 and an uninhibited learning capacity.

Eric's refusal to go to school began in the last weeks of the summer term in his junior school. It coincided with his mother's decision to go out to work, which meant that he would have to eat at school. After she had been out to work for three days, Eric came home from school during the morning and rang her at work in a state of anxiety, asking her to return home at once. He said he felt sick and was afraid of vomiting. Everything was tried to convince him to return, but without success. The mother gave up her work. After the summer holidays, when Eric was due to enter grammar school, he went there only once and was unable to return. For the greater part of the following year he could not leave his mother, even within the house. He said that two things had upset him most on the first day at the new school: all the new boys were shown the sickroom, and from his classroom he could see the cemetery.

Eric was pale and thin; at moments of anxiety—and there were many—he looked ill. His mother was a small, talkative woman; her appearance varied strikingly with her changing moods: she could look gay, carefully dressed in bright colours, or look miserable and uncared for, in either case attracting attention to her state of mind.

She was the daughter of a second-hand clothes merchant in the East End, who contracted Parkinsonism when Mrs A was five years old, became progressively incapacitated, and died when she was 20 years old. During all these years, Mrs A's mother nursed him with great devotion, though she was said to have dominated him. From the description it appeared that Mrs A's mother, too, had had intense hypochondriacal fears about herself and her children. She committed suicide when Eric's mother was in her late twenties. Mrs A had a brother, three years younger, who died in infancy, and another brother five years younger, with whom she has always had an exceptionally close relationship.

Eric's inability to separate from his mother and the concern that mother and son shared about his state of health were obvious at once to whoever saw them at the Clinic. The other striking feature was the undisguised hostility that broke through in their dealings with each other, and which the mother did not conceal in giving his history.

She was able to say that she had not wanted him, had tried to abort him and had been desperate about her failure to do so. She gave a vivid description of the hostility she had felt against him from the start, and of her attempts to suppress his early signs of aggression and unruliness. Her growing failure to do so had led to mutual physical attacks, in which he gained the upper hand from the age of four, when he was able to hurt her so much that she stopped hitting him. Open hostility, anger about his stubborn refusal to comply with her wishes, alternating with anxiety about his health, were the dominant feelings she conveyed to the Clinic staff in her first contacts.

With regard to her husband, two statements characterized her feelings: that he was below her socially, a workman (while her father had been a salesman); and that he had a thumb missing. This need to denigrate him, to deny his masculinity and to treat him as a powerless, useless being was intense. In fact, he was a skilled workman, earned well, but submitted to her ruling in silence. He expressed disappointments about the boy and felt helpless about Eric's and his mother's troubles.

Her need to keep control over her boy's developing powers of independent action and over his masculinity will be shown in detail.

The boy's overt behaviour to his mother, for much of the time, can best be characterized by the word 'ruthless'; and ruthless he was in the treatment of his therapist whenever she stood for the dangerous aspect of the mother. He demanded, threatened and attempted to hurt her physically. He also showed the total lack of concern that is characteristic of ruthlessness and never attempted to make good the damage he had done. He was unable to experience guilt. When his demandingness, destructive and sadistic fantasies reached an intolerable degree, he collapsed into physical exhaustion, bodily pain and hypochondriacal fears. In the sessions he lay on the couch or floor, looking ill, overwhelmed by his fear of illness and death. His fears centred on the dread of having eaten harmful food or having been infected by germs, especially polio. After outbursts of sadistic fantasies in the session in the form of games or actions, he was at times pursued by ghosts that made him run at great speed down the Clinic road to escape them—or, rather, his therapist's fantasied vengeance. For a long time, he brought his sane, active and creative part into the treatment only when he transferred to the therapist the quiet, constructive aspects of the father. The need to keep this island of safety made him tenaciously maintain a one-sided positive image of the father; he denied that there existed a frightening aspect of the father as well as his own aggressive impulses against him, though his nightmares showed them clearly from the start.

The decision to offer the mother treatment came three months after Eric had started. Work with him over these three months had added to the initial observations of the mother gained in superficial contacts with her. There were now clear indications of the areas in which her own disturbance seemed to be deeply linked with his. They centred around his food intake and digestion, the dangers threatening his health and life and her role in his oedipal situation.

Mrs A accepted the offer of treatment reluctantly, making it clear that she had no need for help but was prepared to do anything for the boy's good. Later she thought of it as a possible cure for her migraine. As could be expected, she proved to be an exceptionally difficult patient, who fought her analyst tenaciously in all ways available to a patient in the analytic setting, especially in regard to coming to appointments regularly and on time. Her analyst's unfailing empathy, his understanding of her deep anxieties and of her depression—which made her turn in panic to attack the external world—slowly led her in the transference to experience good feelings in herself and to see the good aspects of her present and past love objects. First experiences of sadness and guilt relating to her dead parents emerged. It was tragic that at this point, when the first tentative loving feelings appeared, she had to experience the loss of her analyst. She did not want to continue with another analyst.

The meaning of food
in the analyses of mother and child

Eric's unceasing demands for time, his insistence on more and more materials to work with, his impatience and despair when his demands were not fulfilled, gave his therapist a vivid experience of his greed and anxiety. At the same time, the absence of belief in mother's safety and goodness and in the therapist's capacity or wish to satisfy him gave evidence of a child in whom anticipation of good, satisfying experiences was lacking. Each good experience remained separate from the preceding one; the next one had to be fought for and forced out of her. Any delay made his anxiety overwhelmingly strong, led to rage and was followed by passivity and sadness.

Food itself formed the centre of his present battles with his mother; demands for special luxury foods that he knew she could ill afford were forced on her. His awareness of her own unconscious conflicts relating to food became clearly visible, and his knowledge of her fear for his survival gave him control over her.

In the mother's own treatment, the analyst experienced her demandingness and aggression and the absence of good expectations. She had dealt with her oral aggression and consequent fear of starvation and emptiness by omnipotently gaining control over food and becoming the person whose power over her objects lay in the food she was giving them or withholding from them. Concurrently, she was haunted by the fear that the food she provided might be harmful and cause a person's death. Her death wishes against a baby brother, born when she was three, who had died soon after birth, had reinforced her belief in her destructive omnipotence. At present, Eric represented the object she fed abundantly, whereas her husband was kept alive on a bare minimum. She could never refuse Eric's extravagant demands, which he repeatedly put in terms of: 'She's got to buy me salmon at sixteen shillings per pound.' The thought that he might eat nothing if she did not fulfil his wishes implied, in her mind, a suicidal threat on his part, which filled her with panic. Her own mother had committed suicide. She felt that she had been totally unaware of her mother's state of mind preceding this event. She was equally unaware of Eric's and other people's sadness, depression and need of support. She was unconsciously expecting a repetition of the suicide experience through Eric. The meaning of suicide and her death wishes against him, especially the attempted abortion, became clear and could be linked with her omnipotent fantasies of her power over life and death through food. Through food she kept him linked to herself and alive; but in break-throughs of her death wishes, she had in fact given him food that she knew was bad.

Eric's fantasies about his mother's good showed that he shared her own omnipotent belief in its power; only her food could keep him alive and through it he remained joined to her. He was unable to eat food she had not prepared; but we found that at the same time he was suspicious of food, feared to be poisoned by her and had to investigate every mouthful. Projection of his oral aggression in his paranoid fears relating to her food clearly played an important part. Later his fantasies led to impregnation fears and passive wishes relating to the father. He identified himself with the suffering woman, and identification with the pregnant woman led to a vivid experience of labour, with pains and exhaustion in the session.

Were we confined to the material from Eric's analysis only, we should have regarded the projection of his oral aggression as the decisive factor in his fear of being poisoned. Our insight into the mother's material, however, has shown us that her unconscious wish to poison him was real and broke through repeatedly. Eric experienced these break-throughs, the anxiety that followed them and the subsequent intensified defenses as an ever-renewed proof that his fear of being poisoned was justified. In this sphere, the problem of communication is not difficult to solve. After meals, when she had given him food that was in fact not fresh or otherwise harmful, her anxieties became intense. She then questioned him repeatedly regarding his digestion, inquired about pos-sible pains, watched him anxiously and, whenever her anxi-ety became too great to tolerate the uncertainty any longer, she gave him one of her many tablets to counteract the fantasied harm she had done. Eric unfailingly took these tablets. He shared all her magic beliefs, he wore articles of her clothing for extra safety, and they took the same tablets to prevent what they anticipated would be the same illness. He even took tablets that had been given to her for menstrual pain. She, in turn, experienced his anxiety and pain as proof that her fantasy of having harmed him was real, and the anxiety he perceived in her confirmed the reality of his own fears.

Both Eric and his mother showed intense anxiety about anything over which they had no power. He expressed this mainly in regard to the weather, the digestive process and germs. An attempt to know details of bodily functioning and illnesses induced in both passing feelings of mastery, but more knowledge brought more threats as well. The magic belief in tablets and their taking of tablets in the wake of fantasied or momentary sensations were a constant feature. Their fantasies of bodily unity became clearest in the simul-taneous experience of pain. They both anticipated and felt it, aggressively projected it onto each other and identified with each other's pain in turn. Only in recent analytic work with Eric does separateness of his bodily sensations begin to appear in relation to his therapist, after a phase of fantasied common experience with her. This gradually brought to an end the magic belief that his and his mother's experiences were one.

In the mother's treatment, similar attempts to extend her pain to the analyst and her wish to have the analyst share her pain with her were observed. The most instructive session in this respect was one in which she desired the analyst to share her menstrual pains, thereby relieving her through the feeling that he, too, suffered, that there no longer was a difference between male and female and that they became joined in this way.

The sexual tie between mother and son

The intensity of Eric's hostility, which appeared undefended in the transference, and the unrestricted indulgence in sadistic fantasies were striking. In these he was for a long time a surgeon who deceived his patients in the hospital, promising them cure but in fact making them suffer the most horrible pain by severing their limbs, skinning them, etc., so that they could never recover. He thereby expressed his suspicion of his therapist and the treatment, projecting his own sadism onto her. He attempted to master his anxiety by himself becoming the sadistic surgeon. Analytic work in this area led to his sadistic intercourse fantasies and to his castration anxiety, which was experienced in these sessions as sudden abdominal pains and anxiety about a possible appendectomy.

His aggressive impulses in rivalry with the father and his fear of the father were strongly defended and remained inaccessible for a long time. Whenever an interpretation had dealt with the sexual aspect of the sadistic fantasies, he stayed away from sessions. This resistance showed that he could talk with comparative ease about killing and torturing, but that the libidinal, sexual aspect of his fantasies was closely guarded. This eventually led to the therapist's conviction that he was guarding a secret.

We later learned about the nature of this secret from the mother's analysis. She gradually became able to admit that her only sexual gratification lay in intensive love play with Eric. She was frigid with her husband and fought against his attempts to have intercourse with her, either by feigning illness or by having the boy in their room. However, she could reach an orgasm by tightly holding and stimulating Eric into complete helplessness. Such scenes began with fights with the excited, struggling boy until he finally was overwhelmed by his excitement and by her physical superiority. At times she pushed her tongue into his mouth.

The origin of this practice can be traced to her primal-scene memories in which fellatio observations or fantasies played an essential part. During or after these early intercourse observations, she had discharged her excitation and rage through masturbation and later by using her younger brother as a partner. In her masturbation fantasies and her sexual games with her brother, she had played the father's role, using her tongue to penetrate. Her horror of being penetrated and of feeling a man on top of her prevented her at times from attending her sessions. When she did come, she attempted to shut out the analyst's words, reversing the roles by attacking him, as she attempted to do in the fight against her husband. The full physical experience of the reversal of roles and of her power to overwhelm her partner were reached with Eric, who now assumed the role Mrs A's brother had played in her childhood. The sex practices with her brother had continued until he reached puberty. When they finally stopped, she became depressed. Later, at the time of his marriage, a prolonged illness brought on by neglect of an ear infection kept her immobilized in the hospital for two years, soon after her father's death. Through this she regained her mother's full attention, who now nursed her with the same devotion that her mother had shown her father.

Fantasies of robbing the analyst of his possessions and a number of acted-out delinquencies against male shop-keepers and ticket collectors revealed the fantasy of robbing her father's penis. These were linked with the father's illness and his gradual deterioration, for which she now felt responsible.

For Mrs A, Eric stood for the brother of her childhood, who had also represented part of herself. The knowledge of this part of her mother's pathology, her sexual practice with Eric and the absence of this material in his treatment made it clear that Eric's overt hostility against the mother had to be understood also in terms of his need to fight her seduction, which doubly threatened him in that he was simultaneously overwhelmed by his impulses and by her body. His fear of being poisoned and of choking can now also be understood in terms of the penetration by her tongue. No differentiated and specific details of these sexual experiences appeared in the transference, but his dread of being overwhelmed by uncon-trollable powers was often experienced in the session. He would then resort to megalomanic mechanisms by which he attempted in fantasy to get control over the powers he feared. The elements, and especially the weather, represented his impulses projected onto the external world, which he sought to control by fantasies of a weather machine.

The reality of his physical experiences with his mother was known to us only from the mother's analysis. In regard to his fear of being poisoned, we found that the understanding and interpretation of his fear of being overwhelmed remained incomplete as long as it was seen only in terms of projection of his own impulses. Being stimulated into help-lessness by his mother and feeling her large body holding him down were real experiences that continued to reinforce his anxiety and counteracted the analytic work in this sphere.

As the analytic work on Eric's dread of his own aggression progressed and he recognized his magic belief in the power of his death wishes, Eric became able to make his first attempts to move away from his mother. He returned to school after one year's analysis, made first contact with other boys, came alone to his sessions but could not yet sleep in his room. Gradually we understood the sequence of fantasies that made it impossible for him to sustain the feeling that he was an independent masculine being. Feeling strong was equal to overwhelming his mother and meant being able to harm her through sadistic intercourse; it also meant being able to attack and kill the father. While working on these feelings in his analysis, he developed a temporary claustrophobic symptom, relating to the headmaster whose sudden death he feared. During the same phase, related problems were worked through: nightmares in which he was facing a bleeding woman with her head cut off; direct attacks on his therapist in which he hurt her 'accidentally' with a knife; and many sadistic fantasies that were followed by regression and withdrawal into illness.

To grow up and become separate meant losing the unity with the omnipotent mother and either being powerless like the father, or powerful and able to harm her. The mother's own omnipotent fantasies were transmitted to him in words and actions. In the oedipal triangle she had far-reaching control over the father. This was an important factor in the boy's inability to separate from her and in his inability to identify himself with the father's masculinity. The sexual secret between mother and son, from which he had to exclude the father and the therapist, had to be guarded because giving it away would bring danger from both mother and father.

So far we have traced the incapacity of mother and son to separate from each other to their sexual tie, the mutual death wishes and their projection. Although the shortness of the mother's analysis did not make extensive work possible, the role of depression—their mutual awareness of it and anxiety about it—was a further important factor in their need to cling to each other. Eric's growing wish for separateness and his turning to the father and teachers had serious repercussions on the mother's state. She experienced Eric's pubertal physical changes and his consequent withdrawal from bodily contact with her as a threat. The realization that she could no longer control his mind and body increased her anxiety, which led to intensification of rages and the need for sexual experiences with him. Both served as a defense against her depression and the feeling of 'nothingness' that she had without him. She could no longer resort to her defense of exhibiting gaiety and excitement and began to feel devalued and unloved. After seeing a film in which a headmaster's wife seduced a schoolboy in order to save him from homosexuality, she felt intensely guilty and for the first time saw Eric as a child she had damaged. Her fight against continuing her sexual play with him led to masturbation with fantasies of an ideal, loving man whom she could love in return and her first loving feelings in the transference. Early in her analysis she recalled feelings of love for her father, but now she experienced her first feelings of mourning for him and guilt about her total lack of conern for him during his long illness and after his death.

After her analyst's death and until the present, there were clear signs of her struggle to let Eric become free from her. She attempted to get satisfaction away from him in line with an earlier fantasy in which she was selling clothes in a large store, thereby outdoing her father who sold secondhand clothes. The crowds and life in the store counteracted her empty and dead inner feelings. At other times she fell back into illness, had minor operations and greatly enjoyed the regressed state of being in bed and cared for by nurses. There were definite signs of pride in some of Eric's excellent school achievements and evident relief about his good physical health. Detailed insight into her fantasies was no longer possible in occasional contacts.

The mother's pathogenic effect

From the material bearing on selected points of interaction in this mother–child couple, certain conclusions regarding the problem of the pathogenic effect of the mother's disturbance on the child can be drawn. Approaching the question from the developmental angle, the following picture emerges.

At birth, Eric met a mother who had no wish to meet him. The available material showed that pregnancy itself was experienced at first as 'the proof that she had lost the battle', as she put it. Her husband had won, had pushed something into her against her will, and she felt compelled to try to do away with it. The baby inside her was felt as an enemy. She projected her own hostility against her pregnant mother onto the baby who in this way stood for the attacking part of herself as well as for her baby brother who died soon after birth. She remembered having reacted with anger to the baby's first movements inside her: she could not control his movements while she carried him.

Immediately after his birth, her fantasies led him to a state of deprivation of basic need fulfillment. When she felt him at the breast, the fantasies of being sucked dry and emptied out by him were uppermost; she experienced feeding as a fight for survival, and her flow of milk remained inadequate. At moments when the sensation of being sucked became pleasurable, the content of what she projected onto the baby changed and her active fellatio fantasies made her abruptly withdraw the nipple. Through these fantasies, Eric was from the start deprived of good satisfying experiences at the breast and felt actual hunger for the first weeks, while the nurses tried to establish breast feeding without the mother's capacity to cooperate. He remained deprived not only of the actual experience of good feeding, but also of bodily contact in general. While he was quite small, the mother's fear of crushing him made her avoid handling him as far as possible. Nor could she allow the father or other people to substitute for her, because she either projected her own impulses onto them or was overcome by sudden feelings of jealousy when she saw the father happily holding Eric, a sight that compelled her to interfere.

A post-partum depression led to withdrawal, inability to eat and consequent loss of weight; her thoughts centred for the first time on her dead mother. She had to watch the baby constantly, never let him out of sight, lest she might suddenly find him dead. This acute fear had an immediate effect also on the early development of his motility. He was kept strapped far more often and much longer than is normal and was given little opportunity to move about freely when he did get on his feet. Thus Eric missed the important elements making for normal development in the early phase: he lacked the experience of good and loving handling and the anticipation of his needs by the mother. These could have led to establishing loving feelings in him, strong enough to mitigate his aggressive impulses and fuse with them, and to the picture of a safe, loving mother in him.

In contrast to the damage done by lack of need fulfillment in the bodily and emotional aspects of his development, there was continued overstimulation of his whole body throughout latency into early puberty. The ultimate damage of such intense sexual stimulation without adequate discharge cannot be estimated from this material, but it is clear that the passive physical experiences with his mother prevented his attempt at establishing his active masculine genitality. Moreover, the anxiety over loss of control was heightened by the fact that the only way open for discharge was through rages. The role of bodily stimulation throughout childhood, and its further impact on problems of identity, have been discussed by Phyllis Greenacre (1958).

The part played by the mother's oral aggression and narcissism and the role of the mother's penis envy and its harmful consequences on Eric will have become clear from the material.

Apart from the content of her fantasies, the damaging effect of the mother's defense mechanisms is of particular importance.

This mother, as has been shown, made of her son an object of projection. Mrs A did not react to the child's needs and impulses on the basis of her perception of his internal situation, but in line with her projections. The overt behaviour and changing needs of the child revived a succession of different infantile conflicts in her. As these became pre-conscious, they brought forth manifestations of her own early anxieties, fantasies and defenses. The child stood successively for aspects of herself and for the different objects of her past in relation to whom she had originally experienced these conflicts.

Moreover, she resorted to omnipotent thoughts whenever she had to admit that she could not know or control people's thoughts and feelings. In relation to her analyst, she denied her wish to know what he felt and thought about her, as well as her curiosity about his private life. Instead, she triumphantly told him 'facts' that she professed to know about him, laying great stress on her 'unfailing intuition'. The facts she knew 'by intuition' were entirely the result of her own wishes and projections. It was particularly striking that she was obviously unable to make use of those perceptions that could have led to a correct knowledge. What she perceived was either not taken in or subsequently distorted when the correct perception would have provoked too great anxiety; for example, she knew 'by intuition' that the analyst was a bachelor. The thought that he might have a wife aroused her intense jealousy and the wish to separate them and attack her. Consequently she did not see facts clearly demonstrating that he was married.

On the basis of this 'intuition' she bypassed the child's needs and forced her own needs in their place. The ensuing inconsistency of the mother's responses to Eric induced in him a constant watchfulness based on the need to anticipate her feelings and actions. In the last phase of his analysis, this watchfulness and his attempt to differentiate his feelings and perceptions from the therapist's became prominent features in the transference. He watched, perceived, and persistently tested his perceptions and their reliability. He had to make sure again and again that she would not suddenly confront him with behaviour for which he was unprepared, that she had feelings that were separate from his. He gradually learned to accept his feelings and perceptions as true and through this experience found his own identity.

The mother's distortion of external reality to which she subjected the child led to faulty reality testing in Eric. We find that the mother's magic thinking, the omnipotent denial she used in order to avoid intolerable facts of external reality, were introjected by Eric, who then operated with her mechanisms in the service of his own defenses. Mother and child experienced his own attempts at reality testing as danger, though for different reasons. For the mother, the danger arose from the fear that the child would force her to face unacceptable facts and attempt to loosen the unity with her. For the child, reality testing and the acceptance of facts that were not in accordance with mother's distorted picture threatened to bring about the loss of unity with her and thus to bear the full brunt of her hostility.

In Eric's case, the distortion pertained particularly to the reality of the father, the image of him as a whole person whose potent and masculine aspects the mother denied. In line with her denial and for the purpose of defense against his anxiety concerning the father, he, too, denied the father's real role. His denial of the real facts in this respect was in turn constantly reinforced by his mother, who thus increased his confusion. For instance, when confronted with Eric's beginning masculinity and his bodily changes, she reacted to his question about his first emission by saying: 'This is nothing special. All men and women have this.'

The mother's beneficient effect

Although this paper is concerned with the pathogenic effect of certain aspects of the close bond between mother and child, I want to bring one example showing a link between an important aspect of his mother's relationship to her own mother, which—in its repetition with Eric—has led to an area in which Eric functions well and can be successful and in which his mother can share his success through identification.

In the early part of his treatment, Eric's capacity to verbalize was severely restricted; words themselves were dangerous. Most of his material was brought in nonverbal ways and through acting. With the progress of his treatment and the gradual disappearance of his persecuting projections, his use of words and the capacity to verbalize increased, and a growing pleasure in beautiful language became apparent. He began to write poetry, and this creative effort led to first experiences of pleasure about his good capacities and to success through appreciation by his teacher.

From the mother's analysis we know that poetry and the wish to speak beautifully had from early childhood formed a strong bond between herself and her mother. This wish had had a defensive quality and had been aimed at warding off their oral aggression. It had signified 'a secret union' against the father, whose crude language had been distasteful to Mrs A's mother. Moreover, 'mother reading poetry to her' had been an actual experience of a peaceful time together, which symbolically stood for good food—food that was given exclusively to her and in which her father and brother had no part.

While Mrs A was unable to give Eric good satisfying feedings, she had repeated with him her own experience of being read to. By reading to Eric, she made him feel her enjoyment of beautiful language. These were, as far as we have seen, the only moments when he could have felt that she was peaceful and when she was able in relation to him to concern herself with something other than his body. Through her double identification—with her own mother who said beautiful words, and with the child who received them from her—she was able to share Eric's enjoyment and progress in this sphere. In other spheres, in which his gifts and activities were derived from his identification with his father, she experienced them as rivalry, and her envy compelled her to interfere with his progress and ruin his enjoyment.

In *New Introductory Lectures* (1933) Freud mentioned the problem of communication of thoughts between mother and child and cited an observation made by Burlingham in which an explanation other than direct thought transference between mother and child could be found for the child's apparent awareness of the content of his mother's thoughts at a given moment. In the concurrent analyses of Eric and his mother I have found no evidence of this, though the fact that I had no direct contact with either patient may be responsible for this. Eric's knowledge of the mother's fantasies, as far as I was able to trace it, could always be related to perceptions of her manifest behaviour in relation to him and the people and objects in the external world around them.

Other investigators have made similar observations. Children whose tie to their mothers is characterized by anxiety and distrust, as in Eric's case, and whose physical bond to her is abnormally prolonged, have also been found to become alert to and remain observant of minute nonverbal clues given unconsciously by their mothers.

Heightened awareness of external perceptions and their interpretation in relation to himself are characteristic of the paranoid patient. When the child's paranoid ideas resulting from his projections meet an external reality that confirms these ideas, when the mother's own destructive or seductive wishes make her not only a fantasied but a real danger, the child clings tenaciously to this watchfulness in relation to her, even after his projections have been understood as such. Only a change within the mother can ultimately free him from this aspect of the abnormal bond and from the real need to protect himself from her.

PART THREE

Problems of adolescence

CHAPTER SEVEN

The psychosexual development in adolescence

T he attempt to condense a complex subject, such as the psychosexual development of adolescents, into a brief presentation can hardly be successful, especially as its complexity and the manifold aspects it presents are the most characteristic features of this subject. I shall therefore not attempt to do more than refer to a few aspects of this phase. My work with adolescents, both in daily life and through their psychoanalytic treatment, has given me the opportunity to observe these developmental problems.

When we ask ourselves why we are so uncertain in our understanding of adolescents and in our approach to them,

Reprinted from J. Hambling and P. Hopkins (eds.), *Psychosomatic Disorders in Adolescents and Young Adults* (London: Pergamon Press, 1965), pp. 35–40.

one answer may lie in the difficulty we experience in seeing the links that exist between the manifestations we observe and the inner conditions from which they derive. Unless we can do so with a measure of certainty, unless we have clues from which we can draw conclusions about what goes on in another person, we are insecure and feel that we have guessed wrong and therefore done the wrong thing. This is just what we are made to feel so often when we deal with boys and girls in puberty and adolescence.

When we say that we understand a child or an adult, this means that we have learned to sense their feelings and to predict their responses.

We are not, on the whole, taken by surprise; we know how to please them, and we can avoid creating painful, frightening or angry reactions. While we know that this is not easy to achieve with very young children, those of us who have spent time and thought on these problems have become more and more secure in our capacity to sense their changing needs and to understand their conflicts and the anxieties resulting from them. If we have watched children grow into school age, we have become aware also of the gradual changes towards harmony and stability. Sudden eruptive behaviour, uncontrollable impulses or immediate demands become rarer or disappear altogether, unless the child is under stress. We say, the child has learnt to cope, and thereby we mean that he has come to establish an equilibrium within himself. He can, as a rule, control his impulses and postpone gratification to some extent. Opposing tendencies become more reconciled, extreme feelings more unified and the anxieties arising from these conditions gradually diminish. A measure of integration has been reached, which gives a picture similar to the one we hope to find at the end of adolescence, when we look out for these features in assessing whether a state of emotional maturity has been reached.

As the children approach puberty and move towards adolescence, few people tell us that life with them remains harmonious. Much of our previous knowledge of them may appear of little use now, and we no longer feel that we understand their reactions, that we can anticipate their wishes or know their tastes. We are no longer sure how we ourselves will be received from one day to the next. We have to try to reassess ourselves and our role again and again in relation to the growing adolescents. Rapid changes of moods and behaviour may be characteristic for a considerable time. Our role may consist in 'just being there', ready to understand and ready to respond, if we are shown that we are wanted, but often ready to accept the signs that we are not wanted just then and certainly not needed in the old way.

With the advent of puberty, when physical and emotional changes begin to upset much of the equilibrium that had been achieved earlier, our task lies in trying to understand the nature and pace of the changes that take place within boys and girls and to try to relate these to the changes of behaviour towards the external world. I can here briefly refer only to some aspects that I consider to be of great importance.

The visible and invisible signs of physical development towards adult sexuality bring new sensations, fantasies and emotions, of an intense nature. The revival of earlier impulses and the need to adjust to and win control over the intensity of the new experiences demand an inner readjustment between the sexual and aggressive impulses and the control over them. A great variety of defensive measures is used in this inner struggle, in order to deal with the anxiety arising during this phase. These have been described with great clarity by Anna Freud (1936), in her book entitled *The Ego and the Mechanisms of Defence*. These defensive measures create the rapidly changing picture presented by adolescents. Were it so that every new step in development were wholly welcome to the child, that growing up and all its implications were wholly acceptable, each new sign of progress would be felt as fulfilment and gradually become part of the personality. In human beings, however, we know that this process cannot usually run smoothly, and that maturation and progress bring conflicts that have to be solved. The comparative freedom from conflicts, or rather the capacity to solve conflicts in ways that do not lead to pathology, are of importance in our attempts to assess normality.

Adolescents who can welcome their physical changes with a good measure of pride, who can allow themselves gradually to derive pleasure from them and whose fears of their new-found capacities are not overwhelmingly strong will go through a phase of anxious fantasying and testing, but gradually they can move forward to the experience and enjoyment of heterosexual relationships emotionally and physically, without being forced back by fear and guilt to regress to earlier forms of physical satisfaction and emotional relationships without being able to establish themselves sexually on the adult level.

Regression plays an important part in the whole process of emotional and instinctual development. The tendency to cling to satisfactions of an earlier phase and a reluctance to exchange these for new and unknown ones, which contain potential dangers, can be observed throughout development. Fluctuations of behaviour at times of stress, illness or tiredness are normal to all of us, and regression becomes pathological only if an arrest of development follows on it. In certain phases of the adolescent process, rapid changes of forward moves and regressive behaviour can be observed. These, too, contribute much to the confusing picture presented to us at times by the young people we are dealing with.

The need to remain on or return to infantile ways of feeling and behaving can be powerfully reinforced by childhood experiences of frustration or over-stimulation. Close knowledge of a child's experiences and detailed studies of parents, their character and psycho-pathology, are being made in many places, aiming at clarification of our understanding of the forces that help or hinder development.

To understand the obstacles on the way to reaching maturity in each individual, detailed knowledge of his development is needed. Much stress has been laid on the part played by revival or recapitulation of earlier inner experiences. In this phase, when the revival of early experiences is joined by the new ones that emerge in adolescence, their slow assimilation produces the varying manifestations we see in the years between puberty and full maturity. Freud has shown early on that needs for bodily satisfaction, in which various bodily zones play their part, undergo certain shifts during childhood. The oral, anal and genital zones play their successive parts on the way to the ultimate organization in which genital experience becomes predominant at the end of adolescence, under normal conditions.

Other elements that contribute to bodily excitation are looking, being looked at, touching and smelling. The role these have played early on, and the fate they have later undergone, are of great importance in the process. The problem of allowing excitation to take its course to the point of discharge is in the centre of the anxieties connected with physical development. They are mostly felt as fears of being harmed or of causing harm to the partner. Where these anxieties remain overwhelmingly strong, they become obstacles to development towards the ultimate normality of adult sexuality.

These conflicting feelings can be observed, for example, in the reactions of boys to their first nocturnal emissions. Few boys experience and few men remember experiencing this event with pure pride and pleasure. The anxieties reported by them lead back to childhood fears and to experiences connected with loss of control over urination and defaecation in childhood. These early fears of loss of control, their connection with messiness and shame, often lead to the need to hide the fact that this much awaited sign of physical maturity has occurred. Aggressive fantasies add to the fear. The first experiences of orgasm also revive earlier anxieties of emotional loss of control, so often connected with rage. Many features of the earlier fate of the boy's masturbation, his sexual and aggressive fantasies and fears, are revived. Now the step has to be taken from experiencing these wishes in fantasy to experiencing passion and discharging it with a real partner.

In girls, the onset of menstruation, the growth of breasts and the sensations and fantasies arising from their physical changes bring conflicts and anxieties that have to be dealt with until a favourable adjustment can be made.

In the last phase of adolescence, it is put to the test whether infantile ways of gratification are so firmly anchored that they interfere with the forward move towards adult sexuality; whether love and aggression were fused sufficiently to combine forces for the sexual act without too great a fear of consequences for the self and the partner; whether taking on the role of man or woman has become possible and an acceptable solution of the bi-sexual conflict within has been reached.

In her paper of 1958, Anna Freud has drawn attention to the fact that it is not sufficient to look at the internal structural changes only in trying to understand the developments in adolescence. The simultaneous need to loosen their infantile attachments, the ties that bind them to the parents, is of great importance and may, where unsuccessfully dealt with, or dealt with by pathological defences, lead to severe pathology. She said, 'There are many adolescents who deal with the anxiety aroused by the very attachment to their infantile objects by simple means of flight. Instead of permitting a process of gradual detachment from the parents to take place, they withdraw their feelings of them suddenly and altogether. This leaves them with a passionate longing for partnership, which they succeed in transferring to the environment outside the family. Here varying solutions can be observed. They may transfer their feelings, needs and phantasies more or less unchanged to parent substitutes. Often these new figures are diametrically opposed in every aspect, personal, social or cultural, to the parents. Or the attachment may be made to so-called leaders, usually persons aged between the adolescent and the parents' generation, who represent ideals. Or passionate ties to contemporaries, either of the same or the opposite sex, are established.' In some adolescents we find that as soon as they feel their growing attachment, especially to an older person, they relinquish this new-found friend again rather than risk experiencing their former dependency. This can create a stage when friendships are broken and new ones formed again and again. This may create a serious problem for establishing the relationship needed for their treatment. At this stage, when treatment of these young people is so important, they may be least likely to profit from it because psychoanalytic treatment is built on the capacity to maintain a close relationship. As soon as the patients begin to have strong feelings for the therapist, they will leave treatment in fear of re-experiencing an infantile attachment.

The physical changes and their repercussions on the inner life of the growing child and the loosening of the ties to the parents have been briefly sketched.

Children who show no signs of inner change or unrest at the age when their contemporaries have shed many features of their earlier school days need our special attention. If, at the age of 15 or 16, they retain all the features of latency children and we are told that they are not interested in things outside the home, that they do not join in 'the silly things' the others in their form are interested in, we have some indications that their development is not progressing normally. Often they do not come to our attention as they do not create problems for their surroundings, but parents or teachers familiar with young people of this age are able to feel that something is amiss.

While they appear to be, and are often referred to, as 'slow developers', some of them may on closer investigation be found to have built up excessively strong barriers against their own impulses early on, and these may be serious obstacles against the normal onset of drive activity in puberty. Unless given help, their development through adolescence into maturity may be severely impaired.

When we think of adolescents reaching maturity, we think of the time when a young man or woman becomes capable of sharing life with a love object of the opposite sex in mental, emotional and physical union. This means that an inner organization has been reached which permits exchanging and not only receiving satisfaction. The capacity to form and maintain relationships must have matured to the point when mutual give and take has won over more primitive forms of relations, over the dependency of the need-fulfilling stage. The capacity to take responsibility, to get pleasure from satisfaction given as well as received, needs a far-reaching change in the inner organization from the time of early dependency on a person.

CHAPTER EIGHT

Observations on adolescents in psychoanalytic treatment

T his contribution is based on observations made in the course of the psychoanalytic treatment of 36 adolescents—24 boys and 12 girls. These are partly cases I have treated and supervised myself; but to a greater extent they relate to material brought together over the past three years by many colleagues and students co-operating in the study of adolescents in treatment at the Hampstead Child Therapy Clinic. The study includes young people between puberty and late adolescence with neurotic or borderline psychotic disturbances. Cases are not included which pre-

---

Paper read at a meeting of the Psychotherapy and Social Psychiatry Section of the R.M.P.A., Autumn, 1961. This study was financed by the Psychoanalytic Research and Development Fund.

Reprinted from *The British Journal of Psychiatry* (May 1964), 110:406–410.

sented a clear picture of delinquent personalities from the outset, though this does not mean that in the course of treatment such features have not appeared. The appearance of impulsive and delinquent features in clinical pictures where we would not expect them in other age groups belongs to the typical experiences and problems of treatment during this phase.

In daily life with adolescents, as in their treatment, we have difficulties in keeping in touch with their inner world and with the repercussions that developmental changes bring about in their relations to the world around them. Our present great need to study and discuss problems of adolescent treatment arises partly from this fact. What adolescents need and what we offer them in treatment are not as closely related as in work with adults and younger children. What adolescents communicate to us about themselves—if they have decided to do so at all—does not consistently enable us to anticipate their next move, to intervene in order to reduce their anxiety in time to forestall the panic that can lead to a breakdown, or to prevent their putting into action the very things they are struggling against. With many adolescents analysis is deprived, to a great extent, of the means of access to the unconscious, on which we rely most in treating children and adults: play is no longer used to convey the continuous stream of phantasies, and free association is resisted until the late stages of adolescence. Communication remains restricted to behaviour and often to carefully censored talk; we become aware that large sections of thought, feelings and daily events have been consistently left outside the treatment, and we may subsequently be faced with considerable surprises.

Such surprises may be due to the fact that we have not yet studied adolescents sufficiently; but a more important reason lies in the nature of the adolescent process itself. Rapidly changing relations between impulses and internal controlling forces and the external world can lead to contradictory behaviour and divergent clinical pictures in rapid succession. Our problem lies in keeping pace with these rapid changes without having been given full insight into the unconscious phantasies and anxieties that have brought them about.

Wide differences exist within the age range we refer to as adolescent patients. The way in which they enter into, make use of and leave treatment differs not only with the nature of their disturbance, but according to the point at which they find themselves in the process of getting acquainted with and winning control over their new bodily sensations and the phantasies deriving from them. In addition, their attempts to detach themselves from their parents and from their internalized aspects have important repercussions in the treatment.

It is helpful to distinguish, on the one hand, between patients whose disturbance has been firmly established from childhood, where the picture in adolescence does not present strikingly unexpected features in spite of intensification of the symptomatology and, on the other hand, patients in whom there was no well-defined neurosis in childhood. These latter have dealt with their anxieties in a variety of ways that have enabled them to go through latency apparently without much trouble, but some time between puberty and adulthood there is an upheaval, unpredictable in form because of the variety of defensive measures that are adopted, discarded again and exchanged for others. While the first group does not present us with specific problems in treatment, at least until they have been freed to enter into the struggle for adolescent independence proper, those whose disturbances appear to be in a state of flux can show rapid changes (e.g. from neurotic to delinquent behaviour, or through a phase of perverse activity into serious withdrawal) which present us with a variety of technical problems (Eissler, 1950). It is, I think, about the latter group we mostly talk in discussions of technical problems.

We can further clarify our understanding of what goes on in terms of both the revival of infantile (pre-genital) drive activity and of new emergent urges and experiences. Both have to be integrated into the existing system, and a new equilibrium has to be established. And at this same time that these far-reaching readjustments have to be made and the conflicts and anxieties deriving from them have to be dealt with, there has to be a loosening of the attachments to the very people around whom their phantasies and intense feelings of love and hate are centring. Attachment to and dependency on the parents must gradually give way till a point is reached which makes it possible for the adolescent to establish his own identity and to find new love objects. These must neither be based too extensively on repetition of the early attachments, nor be too diametrically opposed to them in hostility and rejection, in order to make favourable adult life possible. This can be achieved only after much upheaval and experimenting.

We get the full repercussions of these simultaneous re-adjustments in the transference. While in content this is not too different from what we experience in adult analysis, there is a difference because of the relative weakness of the adolescent ego; the existing real dependency on the parents and the intensity of longing to return to or remain in the earlier position represent a far greater threat for adolescents than for adults.

It is essentially from the aspect of this process of detachment from their infantile love objects and its repercussions in the transference that I shall now approach some technical problems:

We can assess the adolescent patient's capacity to enter into and remain in treatment from the point of view of his capacity to feel and admit that the conflicts that disturb him are located within him, and that he needs help to solve an inner struggle. Such insight, whether it exists when we first meet him or has to be brought about in an introductory phase of his treatment, can carry him through the analytic work; but it may give way before our aim is achieved, according to the nature of his object relationships on entering treatment and the solutions he now tries to find in freeing himself from the bond to his parents. The defensive methods by which various adolescents deal with the anxiety aroused by these bonds and their need to break them in the struggle for their own identity can threaten the relationship to the analyst as well. Heightened anxiety and guilt make massive defensive measures necessary, and an important aspect of our work with adolescents centres on following these successive attempts and failures that produce frequent and rapid changes of behaviour in relation to the analyst.

This makes itself felt already in our first contacts. We constantly meet boys and girls in a state of defiance, who reject their parents and all they stand for. Therefore, they refuse to enter treatment to which their parents try to introduce them. If we succeed in getting them to attend, treatment may be successful at first, often on the basis of their phantasy that they have found an ally against their parents, whereby in their minds they make us entirely good and their parents entirely bad. When this is pointed out, the defiance can quickly turn against the analyst. Technically one should be able to deal with it, as one does when it occurs in patients of other ages; but all one's capacity and skill may be useless, simply because the patient breaks off treatment at this point. Such adolescent boys and girls attempt to find freedom from the internalized and from the external parents by turning love into hate, or dependence into revolt. The freedom resulting from this does not go far; they remain in fact closely attached and soon experience guilt and suffering, which lead to further increase in defensive measures.

Where projection is used extensively, the parents and the analyst may turn into persecutors. Suspiciousness in the transference, as a passing phase, can easily turn, with increased projections, into paranoid behaviour; and again the problem, difficult as it may be, can be successfully dealt with only if the patient is able to come and face the dreaded analyst at all. But this is exactly what seems too difficult for many of them.

There is another type of adolescent patient, often around the middle years, who makes us feel at first that he has fewer problems and is likely to benefit from treatment. He seems eager to come, he asks for help, and he shows a good measure of insight into his disturbance. He comes punctually on the appointed day, and five days a week he talks about his troubles and phantasies, his daily life, his ideas about the world and his hopes for the future. He behaves towards the analyst as to a friend he has long waited for and found at last. But this initial rosy picture tends to change as soon as the analyst does his job and analyses and does not conform in reality to the role that has been attributed to him in phantasy.

Analysis of the transference nature of their feelings and of defensive elements in them, and especially of the infantile aspects underlying them, quickly brings clouds into the picture. Much depends on the existing ego strength of the moment whether in spite of frustrations in the transference the patient will stay on and co-operate or will, at least temporarily, relinquish the tie to the analyst that was built on such insecure ground.

If we try to see the point in the course of the process of detachment from his parents at which we have entered the adolescent's life, we may find that he had just arrived at a measure of freedom from them by shifting the positive feelings from them to us. The shift, so well known in the form of the 'crush' on the teacher or youth leader, has reached the analyst. Idealization, the wish for closeness to a new object, the need for identification and admiration are all to be found in these first positive moves. In daily life during this phase, when the admired adult falls short of the hopes set on him, the relationship is broken and the feelings moved to a new person. The repercussion of this *need to exchange love objects*, which in itself is a normal phase, can present a subtle technical problem during treatment: the attachment to the analyst may not prove sufficiently strong to carry the patient through the frustrations of analysing the infantile and defensive elements of his feelings—and he leaves.

Yet another problem we have encountered is the following. Where analysis proceeds satisfactorily, we come to a
point when intense infantile feelings are re-experienced in
the transference. As the patient's dependence on the analyst
grows and he regresses, we may find, especially in the early
and middle years of adolescence, a strong reaction against
experiencing regression, whereby the further emergence of
infantile feelings is evaded. Eruptive aggressive behaviour
against the analyst, or acting out and asserting 'grownup-
ness' by sexual experiences with yet another boy or girl, may
appear at the very time when babylike separation anxiety,
the need to be taken care of and tender feelings are beginning
to be felt towards the analyst. Such a regressive phase is
painful at all ages, but a favourable therapeutic outcome
depends on it. Once he reaches it, the adolescent who may
have been progressing well in his treatment may now be
compelled to muster all his defences so as to counteract *the
fear of ego regression,* the fear of losing his intellectual and
creative achievements and losing touch with reality. The
threat of losing what independence and separateness he has
achieved seems more intense where the patient finds himself
only just on the threshold of establishing his identity.

Boys who have been fixated to their mothers long beyond
the normal time and have experienced direct bodily care and
satisfaction from them through latency and into puberty
present a special problem. Their demanding, dependent relationship is quickly transferred to the analyst; but forward
movement into more advanced stages of object relationship
is established in them only with great difficulty. I see two
main reasons for this: genital urges and phantasies are
especially frightening when the mother has remained so
close to their bodily experience and where her actual
behaviour is seductive towards the adolescent boy rather
than restrictive. Clinging to baby ways in relation to her, to
her food and her care in illness, with aggression expressed
in infantile ways, is maintained or reverted to as a safe-
guard against emerging masculine sexual and aggressive
wishes.

A move forward and to a new object runs up against another difficulty in these cases. There is a *fear of the mother's depression or of her breakdown or of her vengeance* on the boy's turning away. The fear of such responses by the mother has a certain basis in reality, powerfully reinforced by past and present hostile wishes against her. Where this manifests itself in the transference, *clinging to the analyst,* in passivity and oral dependency, reappears again and again, and in these cases the decisive moves are made only in late adolescence and after very long analyses, when the mothers also have been helped to find a solution for their problems in relinquishing the tie to their sons.

Patients who either start their treatment or later arrive at the point where the analyst becomes the centre of hetero- or homosexual feelings experience serious difficulties, especially where the actual person of the analyst is not too remote in age and sex from the most intense wishes of the moment. The *anxiety caused by experiencing sexual feelings in the sessions,* the fear of having erections and losing control are at the back of many silences, apparent boredom and absenteeism. Again the problem itself is well known to us, but the intensity of the fear of losing control and the increased narcissism that makes rejection and frustration so especially difficult to stand in adolescence can create a more serious impasse here.

The question of termination of adolescent treatment can be clarified if also approached from the angle of growing detachment and separateness. The *wish to feel free from the analyst* often appears well before we feel safe about the patient's capacity to make this step. It seems important to differentiate here between a state that looks like resistance but may—at this stage—contain important elements of normality and health. Where this is recognized we have found that successful work, where integration had been almost reached, has made it possible for adolescents to return to their analyst later, of their own accord, either to continue work that they felt to have been incomplete or to report on their good experiences and let their analyst share in them. From such adolescents who return as young adults we can learn a great deal, especially about the problems that they have been compelled to keep outside the analysis earlier on, and about the reasons for it.

These examples may have shown among other things that *adolescent patients can, in fact, rarely fulfil the basic requirements of psychoanalytic treatment for any length of time.* Regular daily attendance, communication of thoughts, feelings and daily events in words, without conscious withholding, the capacity to maintain the relationship with the analyst through its changing and frustrating experiences are the basic elements on which psychoanalysis rests. But they are also the very elements that, at some time or other, if not throughout adolescence, are diametrically opposed to what adolescents want and can tolerate.

The part played by the adolescent's parents during treatment, and our role in relation to them, should be referred to. As we see the main goal of adolescence as the achievement of independence based on the subject finding his own identity and the capacity for heterosexual love and creativity, it is clear that treatment that aims at helping him towards this goal must be his own. He must feel that his analyst and his treatment are *his* concern. For many, the thought of their parents' part in it destroys the very hopes they have set on the treatment. This does not mean, however, that parents of adolescent patients do not need help. On the contrary, it seems more true to say that most parents of adolescents go through a phase when they need some guidance or support. Parents of a child who is ill enough to need treatment are likely to be people who react to some or all manifestations of the child's leaving them with a revival of their own conflicts, and this is bound to affect the process of detachment. The analysis of mothers and fathers of children during this phase shows us constantly the variety of feelings that are evoked in them. To enumerate only a few we have met, there is first the mother's feeling of loss, as a response to her child's wish to free himself, and with that the whole range of depressive, hopeless or angry feelings according to what loss has meant to her early on and throughout life. Or she may cling to the child, make him feel guilty and anxious and thereby interfere with his first tentative attempts to move out of the close bond. Or there may be a need to prevent, to share in or to compete in the first love relationship; an ambition to push the adolescent into a life that the parent has failed to make a success of; or on the contrary, envy of his achievements and destructive interference each time the child has achieved success that was out of the parents' reach. The subtle shades of interplay during this time, by which the adolescent's struggle can be helped or hindered, are seen especially clearly where we have the opportunity to look into the analysis of parent and child simultaneously.

It is, of course, the task of the adolescent's own therapist to deal with his reactions to the parents. We know, however, that where parents are severely pathological, and especially in this vulnerable phase, persistent onslaughts against the tenuous, growing feelings towards an independent self or the over-taxing of the weak capacity to control overwhelming impulses may be such that the struggle is given up, and massive pathological defences establish themselves at a point when the way out of illness seems within reach.

To deal with the parents' need for help in practice mostly requires someone other than the adolescent's analyst and, where possible, a place other than the adolescent's clinic. In a later stage of a successful analysis, adolescent patients are able to differentiate between their own and their parents' problems more clearly, and it is at this stage that I have met with a boy's and a girl's well-founded and well-received suggestion to their mothers that the ultimate success could be reached more safely if the mother sought help for herself.

A brief contribution to a topic of great complexity is bound to raise more problems than it can answer. It may, however, achieve the aim of highlighting some of them and of characterizing the special ways in which we attempt to find solutions.

Conclusion

The great variety of problems met with in the psychoanalytic treatment of patients in the years between puberty and adulthood has been discussed. They have been related to the main developmental changes that occur in this phase; the re-arrangement of the equilibrium between impulses and controlling forces, as well as the changing relations to the adult world, bring about temporary disturbances that make the analyst's intervention more threatening than at earlier or later stages.

The capacity to enter into the adolescent patient's world, to respond to his changing needs and to retain his trust is a pre-requisite for successful treatment at this stage. The number of analysts who feel able to deal with patients in this age group remains comparatively small.

Those whose interest in these special problems and whose gifts have enabled them to gather experience find that the value of psychoanalytic work with young patients is great. It lies not only in the therapeutic possibilities, but in the preventive role analysis can play at this stage, forestalling the establishment of sexual deviations and of a choice of partner made on the basis of the adolescent's psychopathology. It also plays a part in preventing entry into a career chosen for neurotic reasons.

CHAPTER NINE

Assessment of analysability illustrated by the case of an adolescent patient

Once the diagnostic assessments of a personality and its psychopathology have been completed, the next step in our diagnostic procedure aims at making a decision regarding the therapeutic intervention most indicated at the present stage. Where we reach the conclusion that psychoanalysis is indicated, the problem of the patient's capacity to make favourable use of this form of treatment poses itself.

Assessment of analysability or treatability has to take into account the presence of factors deriving from all parts of the personality structure. It is the combination of factors and their interplay that present the main problems of evaluation and point to the roles the pathological versus the intact

Reprinted from *Bulletin of the Philadelphia Association for Psychoanalysis* (1964):14; *Bulletin of the Hampstead Clinic* (1978), 1:65–73.

aspects of the personality will be likely to play in the course of treatment. In children and adolescents, age and the developmental stages reached are of particular importance in assessing treatability.

Assessment of treatability in adolescence

The problem of deciding whether and when psychoanalytic treatment can profitably be entered and made use of is of special interest in adolescence, when certain elements of the treatment situation have been found to be especially difficult to tolerate in certain phases of the adolescent process. If it were possible to ascertain at the time of referral that co-operation is likely to be particularly difficult for the young patient at this point and that there are good reasons to presume that he could make better use of treatment at a later stage of adolescence, it would be of great advantage to decide postponement, unless an immediate crisis situation exists. Entry into treatment under unfavourable external or internal conditions needs to be avoided in adolescence also, because the fragile inner balance can be adversely affected by it at certain points in the process of inner re-arrangement; therefore the capacity to detect these at the initial stage is of great advantage. Further, it is important to maintain in the adolescent the feeling that psychoanalysis is a therapy to which he can return in adult life, should the need arise, and therefore experiences of great anxiety or of being unwillingly made to undergo treatment leading to a hostile turn against it should be avoided.

The following material is taken from a detailed study of the repercussions of the adolescent changes on the capacity to co-operate in analysis, as it has been carried out at the Hampstead Clinic. The study has increased our understanding of the problem of spotting potentially unfavourable conditions at the initial stage and has helped us to clarify certain constellations of factors that make the analyst's entry into the life of adolescent patients comparatively more acceptable to them. We take the view at the Clinic that the 'therapeutic alliance' is a prerequisite for successful treatment of adolescents. I attempt in this paper to show the need to look for all elements that appear to help or hinder the process of analysis and to detect them at the diagnostic stage. Further, I compare the initial assessment in this respect with findings in the course of treatment, and make a final assessment at the time of termination.

Assessment of analysability at the diagnostic stage

Material studied at the diagnostic stage, between the patient's referral and the completion of the diagnostic assessment, consists of the social history gathered by the Psychiatric Social Worker in interviews with the parents and where possible with other members of the family. It includes the patient's interview or interviews with the psychiatrist in charge of his diagnostic assessment; the patient's intelligence test carried out by the psychologist; information reaching the Clinic from other sources, e.g. information from the family doctor and school. This material allows us to detect the presence or absence of factors that we consider to be basic prerequisites for the capacity to profit from psychoanalytic treatment. Not all of these are clearly visible initially, according to the patient's psychopathology, but a picture of his personality structure and of the level of his object relationships can be gained on this basis and gives us valuable indications.

It is clear, however, that a number of additional factors necessary for the attempt to assess analysability cannot be reached through the diagnostic material. These do not emerge until the patient is experiencing the treatment situation proper, and until at least his first reactions to the main elements of the analytic situation become observable.

Freud regarded a provisional beginning of analysis as the only adequate way of arriving at a conclusion about the patient's capacity to profit from analytic treatment and suggested using the first one or two weeks as a period of observation. In our study, the material gained at the diagnostic stage was added to material from the first treatment sessions. The number of sessions needed for the purpose of evaluating the adolescent patient's reaction to the treatment situation varied considerably according to the nature of the defences appearing in the initial phase, and according to the nature of the fantasies transferred in the initial phase, both of these being factors felt to be relevant for prediction.

Clinical illustration: the case of George

The case of a boy aged 13 years 5 months at the time of referral is used here to illustrate the work of assessment. The interviews on which assessment was based were recorded immediately after they had taken place.

Referral symptoms

At the time of referral George was a small, thin boy. He was pale, had a worried look and at the age of 13½ years did not look more than 11 years old. He was referred because he had a very disturbing symptom; he suffered intense anxiety at the moment of defaecation, thinking that his faeces would remain stuck. He spent almost an hour on the lavatory morning and evening and was very preoccupied with lavatories and with cleanliness. His symptom was especially disturbing to him during holidays, as he could not know in advance where he would find a suitable lavatory. In addition to this symptom he showed other disturbances: he had withdrawn from his friends and spent most of his time playing on his own. He also seemed intensely jealous of his brother, four years older than himself. In spite of an IQ of 142, he did badly at school and disliked going there.

Assessment based on motives for referral

> *Comment*: In patients of all ages, the motivations for seeking treatment need careful consideration when one attempts to evaluate their capacity to co-operate in psychoanalytic work. Experience has shown that where essentially external reasons and pressure have led the patient to seek treatment and where there is little evidence of his capacity to feel that his inner situation is responsible for the problems he is experiencing, analytic work encounters serious obstacles. In such cases considerable time is needed until it becomes clear whether such awareness can be brought about. While in adult cases this situation is usually confined to certain psychopathologies, as in delinquents (where either courts of law or persons in the immediate surroundings exert pressure), children and adolescents are nearly always referred in the first place because their parents or the school authorities have decided that treatment must be sought. The motives leading parents to this decision and their attitude to their child's treatment must therefore form part of the assessment in every case.

It will be shown here how potentially favourable and unfavourable elements in the external setting were evaluated at the time of George's referral.

Mother's motives for referral and attitude to treatment

(a) Initial assessment

George's mother was familiar with psychoanalytic treatment; she had a brief experience of it herself, and George's older brother had three years of analysis at the Hampstead Clinic, with favourable results. The family had therefore maintained a positive attitude to the Clinic.

> *Comment*: This situation can be considered to be essentially favourable as a basis for referral of a second child in the family, especially as the treatment of the first child has given the opportunity to ascertain that neither parent's ambivalence to the treatment and the analyst had formed a serious obstacle to the boy's treatment. Nevertheless a number of potentially unfavourable factors arising from the mother's psychopathology had to be considered in George's case.

Although the mother was interested in and well disposed towards analysis, she had terminated her own treatment after a short time saying that she had undertaken it only because of her intellectual interest in it. A number of years had elapsed and it had become clear in recent contacts with her that her tendency to fall ill and her numerous hypochondriacal fears had become more marked. There was no evidence that she had insight into the possibility of a link between her physical ailments and a psychological basis for them. Moreover, it became clear in the interviews with her that her hypochondriacal concern was not confined to herself, but that it extended to George's body, and that a close body-relationship still existed between her and him. Although a similar situation had existed between her and the older boy, there was no doubt that her feeling of physical unity with George was more intense.

> *Comment*: Experience with cases of this age group, where similar conditions were found, has shown these to contain serious obstacles to treatment owing to the primitive tie between the mother and her adolescent son and her incapacity to loosen it without undergoing treatment.
>
> Difficulties tend to arise when the analysis of the adolescent has successfully dealt with obstacles against his forward move, and the mother counteracts his attempts to

free himself from his infantile bond as she experiences his growing independence as a loss of satisfaction.

The possibility of such interference in George's treatment had to be taken into account as a potential danger. It is impossible, however, to evaluate the intensity of the mother's need to maintain the relationship on this level and to predict the mechanisms she will use when faced with the conflict. Guilt about the nature of her relationship with him had to be considered as one of the motives for referral and potentially as a factor helpful to his treatment.

(b) *Mother's role seen during treatment*

In the first part of the treatment the nature of the relationship between George and his mother proved in fact to be pathologically close and related to bodily experiences. He shared with her the concern about his health, and they both directed much of their attention to their own and each other's state, which was expressed in the persistent taking of temperatures. This led to repeated absences from his treatment. During a separation from his mother who had gone away to nurse her own mother, George stayed in bed for two weeks. On her return the mother spontaneously considered the possibility that this might have been a reaction to her absence and said that 'she would hate to think that he might still be so dependent on her'. At this point she reasserted her wish that he should have treatment. In the tenth week of treatment, however, the mother arranged for herself and George to enter hospital at the same time. She was to have a minor breast operation and he an appendectomy. She did not consult the therapist before making these arrangements, and there did not seem to be a clear reason for George's appendectomy. Attempts to keep George at home and away from sessions on various pretexts also occurred in the first half-year of treatment. With George's growing positive attachment to his therapist and the analysis of the defensive aspect of his regression and of his continued clinging to his mother, he showed the first active move towards independence. From

then onwards and throughout his further treatment it
became obvious that his mother was able to gain satisfaction
from many of his new achievements. She was relieved about
the disappearance of his symptom, and there was no evidence
in his treatment that she actively interfered with his progress. We gained the impression that she became more concerned with her own health than she had been before.

One aspect of the mother's relationship to George seemed
to have a helpful influence on his capacity to communicate in
treatment. This was the interchange of observations about
themselves that had existed between them. While originally
centred on observations of bodily functions, the analysis
showed that enjoyable, good talks between them had moved
on to different subjects and that George had brought the
experience of talking as a helpful enjoyable experience into
the analysis.

The father's role

(a)   Initial assessment

In George's referral, as in his older brother's treatment, the
father retained the role of an outsider. His attitude was
ambivalent; he refused to be involved and let his wife take
the decision. When he attended the Clinic once, he made the
impression of a responsible man who provides well for his
family's material needs but who does not actively participate
in taking decisions. He seemed satisfied with the older son's
progress following his treatment and was puzzled by
George's symptom. While he could not be considered as a
helpful factor in George's treatment, there seemed no reason
to expect any interference from him.

(b)   Assessment during treatment

The assessment of the role the father would be likely to play
proved to be correct. He did not wish to participate by seeing

the therapist, nor did he interfere by making George's attendance difficult or making disparaging remarks. He played a
positive role, however, in counteracting the mother's tendency to keep George at home because of some imaginary
illness.

George's motivations for wanting treatment

(a) *Initial assessment*

Suffering caused by his symptom: George spontaneously
expressed his wish to have treatment. The main reason for
this wish and its urgency lay in the nature of the symptom. It
caused him a great deal of discomfort and anxiety and interfered more and more with his life. At the time of referral he
was particularly concerned that it would interfere with the
family's plans for the coming summer holidays.

> *Comment*: The degree of suffering caused by a symptom
> always plays an important part in a patient's initial readi-
> ness to undergo treatment. This alone cannot, however, be
> regarded as a sufficiently strong motive to carry it
> through. In cases where an early shift and the disap-
> pearance of the symptom occurs, treatment is endangered
> unless awareness of the need to deal with the conflict
> underlying symptom formation is present, and where
> other disturbed aspects of the personality are not recog-
> nized by the patient.

*Awareness of lack of age-adequate functioning and
fears*: The wish to free himself from his anal symptom was
not the only reason why George felt that he needed treatment. In the course of the first interviews he mentioned the
following additional motives for wanting help: that he was
afraid of other boys, that he could not play games and had
withdrawn increasingly during the last year; that he felt
lonely; that, comparing himself with others of his age he felt

small and childish (he admitted taking toy animals to bed); that he was disturbed by his school failure.

(b)   *Assessment during treatment*

George's main symptom, the poking of faeces from his anus, disappeared after nine months, before its meaning was fully understood. By that time George's wish to free himself from his anxieties, to grow up, have friends and learn well was in the foreground, and his attachment to his therapist so strong that there was no danger of insufficient motivation. Throughout anxious and resistant phases, George's wish to use the therapist for the purpose of becoming manly remained prominent and re-emerged as the leading motive whenever passive wishes temporarily seemed to submerge it.

Evaluation of potentially positive and negative factors in George's personality, as seen in his diagnostic interviews

Intelligence and verbalization

The fact that George has good intelligence (IQ = 142) was seen to be of positive value, although we know that intelligence does not, in itself, allow us to predict that the patient will make good use of his treatment. The combination of George's excellent intelligence with other factors seen at the diagnostic stage made it seem likely, however, that one could expect favourable contributions from this constellation: he combined with his intelligence an unusually good capacity to verbalize and to communicate internal experiences in words. There was a quality in his communications that showed his search for causal connections and a strong urge to clarify them. It was clear from the material of his first treatment sessions that putting thoughts and feelings into words and finding links gave him satisfaction.

> *Comment*:   Verbalization and the facility to talk in diagnostic or analytic sessions cannot in itself be regarded as a favourable factor, although the absence of this capacity makes treatment difficult, if not impossible. Although it is not easily recognized initially, the defensive use made of speech has to be taken into account in the evaluation. Especially in adolescence, intellectualization tends to be used extensively and the flow of speech thus becomes an obstacle.

Verbalization and object relationship

George showed clearly that one aspect of his eagerness to communicate about himself was derived from his wish to form a relationship with his therapist, and he used various ways to make this clear to him. He not only described parents, brothers and teachers but brought photographs of them, saying: 'You must get to know them all'. He also referred to special words he uses and said: 'You must learn my private language'. His verbal communications aimed at being understood, and at introducing the therapist into his world.

> *Comment*:   This is an unusually favourable situation at the beginning of treatment at George's age. It may, however, be prompted by elements not visible at this initial stage and cannot therefore be taken as a secure basis for prognosis of analysability.

Verbalization and exhibitionism

In addition to the evident pleasure in putting thoughts into words, which had a sublimatory quality, and the use of speech in its function of communication aiming at establishing object relationships, George's speech itself and the content of some of his communications had an exhibitionistic quality. Showing his good capacity to speak could be regarded as pleasure in demonstrating his intellectual ability, but most of the content of his talk was aimed at exhibiting his defects. This combination, through which he aimed at getting masochistic gratification, appeared likely to counteract progressive trends in the analytic work. While the presence of this combination of factors was noted, the comparative strength and ultimate influence on the therapeutic progress could not be foretold.

The role of verbalization during treatment

During his treatment the picture shown initially remained unaltered with regard to the use George made of verbalization. Even in the phases of strong resistance he was able to put the conflict into words. His acting in the transference remained confined to non-verbal communications via changed posture, facial expression or hand movements. In the first year he missed sessions owing to his hypochondriacal fears and conversion symptoms, but unlike other adolescents he did not stay away in order to avoid putting thoughts and feelings into words. George's need to maintain the relationship to the therapist was prominent throughout and he remained able to communicate both his aggression and his positive feelings in words.

The exhibitionistic aspect of his use of speech that had been evident at the diagnostic stage also proved to play an important part in later stages of his treatment. While early on its main function was the display of his defects, analysis of the masochistic and the defensive aspects of his exhibitionism led to his using speech to show his achievements and capacities. The use of subtle shades of verbal expression, wit and quick dialogue became remarkable features in the analytic sessions and contained the aggressive and competitive

aspects of the therapist's empathy and the response to interpretation that brought hitherto defended thoughts and feelings into consciousness.

Self-observation and self-criticism

From all that has been said so far, it will have become clear
that the self-observing function of George's personality was
well developed and remarkably free from interference in its
functioning. He also gave evidence of self-criticism at the
diagnostic stage, expressing his discontent with himself in
comparison with his contemporaries.

> *Comment*:   The ego's function of self-observation is a pre-
> requisite for psychoanalytic treatment. Where this capa-
> city is not available, analytic work proper cannot be car-
> ried out. Only after a considerable observation time does it
> become possible to determine whether a patient will be
> able to develop this capacity within the analytic setting,
> on the basis of identification with the analyst whose obser-
> vation he may be able to take in and make use of.
>
> Where we find the self-observing function present, it
> cannot in itself be regarded as a factor that allows us to
> predict favourable contributions to treatment. Only in
> combination with certain other features does the positive
> contribution of the self-observing function make itself felt;
> in combination with other factors it may come to form an
> obstacle to therapeutic work, as e.g. when we find it com-
> bined with strong narcissistic or masochistic trends.

In George we found indications of the presence of such
unfavourable elements. They became visible especially in
his concern about his body and its functions, and the concern
about his health. At the diagnostic stage it was impossible to
foretell the intensity of these needs and the possible interference they would present with his progress. Other features
were noted, however, which appeared to augur well for the

contribution they could make to the therapeutic work, in conjunction with George's well functioning self-observation.

Self-criticism and the presence of an ideal self

One aspect of George's superego manifested itself clearly at the initial stage: this was the presence of an 'ideal self', of a conscious picture of the 'self-he-would-like-to-be'. George expressed discontent about himself, his childishness and poor work. His wish to change and to be helped to reach a stage that he would feel to be appropriate for a boy of his age was seen as a positive factor in the evaluation of his analysability.

> *Comment*:   The existence of an appropriate or potential ideal self that promotes the wish to seek help must be regarded as one of the pre-requisites for successful treatment, on which the continued effort and active participation are built. In many cases this is not clearly visible initially. However, the existence of an ideal self and a wish to change cannot, in themselves, tell us the extent to which they will in fact contribute to the analytic work, unless we can trace other elements in the patient's personality that will show that they are likely to support the 'working towards the goal' set by the ideal self.
>
> The capacity to test the reality of the features in the self in relation to the ideal self is of importance here. At the diagnostic stage this can help us to make a distinction between the patient's wish to get treatment essentially for reality-adapted reasons that are within his reach, or whether his expectations from treatment are largely built on fantasies, whose function it is to deal with anxiety and whose link with reality is a very tenuous one. Where the latter is the case, each sign of progress may lead to disappointment through the realization that the ideal self remains out of reach, while, on the contrary, awareness of progress leads to the wish for further work, where bridg-

ing the distance between the wished-for self and the real self lies within the realm of possible real achievement.

In the course of George's treatment it was possible to follow the dynamic changes that took place between the conflicting forces within his personality and to evaluate their changing effect on the capacity for active participation. As expected, the favourable aspects of the ego's contribution were strongly counteracted by George's narcissistic and masochistic features. During the first year the impression was confirmed that much of his self-observation was given to satisfying these needs, which also served the purpose of maintaining the close bond to the mother. The analysis of the defensive aspects of his passivity and his self-injuring tendencies brought about a marked change in the second year, and from then onwards the factors seen initially as potentially favourable gained in strength. Through the growing relationship with the therapist George became able to use his intelligence and the self-observing function of his ego more and more in the service of his treatment, gradually taking an active part in what he termed 'the detective work'.

George's ideal self did not contain significant fantasy elements, nor was there evidence throughout the treatment that he thought of achieving his aim of becoming masculine by magic means. He was convinced that he could reach his goal only with the help of a man, i.e. by identification, and it was possible to analyse the various aspects of this idea and to detect in it the successive steps from passive submission, then to the borrowing of strength, and finally the awareness of the strength in himself that allowed him to face the therapist as well as his brother and father in competition.

The conflict of activity versus passivity

The question of whether George would be able to muster the strength for active participation necessary for treatment posed itself initially in view of his marked retreat into passivity over the last years. In spite of his conscious wish to move forward, the regressive pull was clearly a strong one. The only indication we had at this early stage of treatment which showed that he was capable of choosing progression rather than regression lay in his own choice of carrying out the treatment by talking rather than by playing (which had at first seemed attractive). As indicated before, the struggle between active and passive strivings in George was very marked during the first year of treatment, when retreat into illness and over-compliant behaviour towards his therapist persistently showed his tendency to retreat and to avoid activity. The severe inhibition of his aggression and his sadistic fantasies came into analysis under great resistance, and he gradually began to move forward and to become active as his fears of his own violence and his castration anxiety were analysed. It became clear also that his capacity to bear frustration was stronger than had appeared originally; it was he who said repeatedly at moments of resistance: 'it's difficult, but it's *got* to be'.

Precursors of transference

Comment: On entering the Clinic, every patient has a picture in his mind of the experience he is about to undergo. It is frequently possible to get clues to the meaning the idea of himself as someone in need of psychiatric help has for him, and to get some insight into his unconscious fantasies relating to this experience. Although the fantasies and feelings are composed of a large number of elements, we can sometimes trace one or the other in the social history, as for example past hospitalizations of the patient himself, nervous breakdowns in the family, etc. The meanings such real experiences have taken on can sometimes become visible through fantasies the patient brings or through defensive behaviour.

The first treatment sessions permit closer evaluation of the nature of the initially transferred features (pre-cursors or transference). Where they present themselves as serious obstacles indicating, for example, that guilt or fear of madness may make the treatment as such overwhelmingly threatening, the analyst can arrive at a clearer picture only through an observation period. This permits him to see whether defence interpretation can sufficiently relieve the initial anxiety on the basis of the scanty material available, or whether the immediate transfer of negative features dooms the analysis to failure at this point.

In George's case, the early transference manifestations led to a positive evaluation in terms of his wish to form a relationship and his trust in the therapist's capacity to help. In studying the material of the first treatment sessions, several questions arose from this positive beginning. George approached the therapist with the conviction that he had found the man who would free him from his anxieties and through whom he would get help in his struggle against his passive and infantile wishes. While this is favourable for the establishment of a therapeutic alliance, it was necessary to keep in mind the great part played by George's castration anxiety which had led to the regression, and to consider that his passivity and his wish to submit to the male therapist might be strong enough to counteract the positive factors. Although George had brought two plasticine figures to the diagnostic interview which he used to demonstrate the persecution of the Jews and whose features gave evidence of his castration anxiety, his treatment did not bring transference aspects of a persecutory nature; nor did it bring fears of his therapist as a castrating figure, which would have disturbed analytic work by their intensity.

Throughout the changing aspects of the transference George remained able to maintain the therapeutic aspect of his relationship to his therapist.

Conclusion

This attempt to choose a number of factors seen in the initial contacts with an adolescent and to base on them a tentative prediction of his capacity to co-operate in psychoanalytic treatment shows, on the one hand, the limitations of our capacity to predict and clarifies, on the other hand, those areas in which our assessments have been well founded. It has become clear that while the presence of certain basic requirements for treatment can be detected or their absence noticed initially, the interplay of forces cannot be predicted with any measure of certainty. We have, however, improved our capacity to assess inner and outer conditions, and this has led to more careful preparation of the patient and his family for the demands treatment will make on them. We hope in this way to arrive gradually at a point where entry into treatment can be more closely related to the patient's capacity to profit from it.

PART FOUR

Other contributions

CHAPTER TEN

Research
in a child guidance clinic

O ur discussions in these last days have amply shown
that there is a great need for research in child guidance and that it has to be planned in many directions
within the scope of our work. In each of the fields we have
mentioned so far—prevention, diagnosis, prognosis and
treatment—and, finally, in the evaluation of all our interventions there are wide areas of speculation and uncertainty. To take the question of prognosis, on whose immense

The content of this paper is based on material collected in the
Hampstead Child-Therapy Clinic, with the aid of grants by The Field
Foundation, Inc., New York, The Foundations' Fund for Research in
Psychiatry, New Haven, Connecticut, The Ford Foundation, New
York, The Psychoanalytic Foundation, Inc., New York, and The Grant
Foundation, Inc., New York, and it was read at the World Health
Organization Seminar on Child Guidance, 29 August to 9 September
1960, Brussels.

value we are all agreed, as an example: we have over the years accumulated a body of knowledge of child development and of the conditions we have found to have favourable and unfavourable consequences on the development of the various aspects of the child's personality and on its relations with the world around him. Long-term studies of the children and their families from birth to adulthood are constantly bringing more knowledge, and, potentially, every case we have the opportunity of investigating brings further evidence. But there are wide areas in which our knowledge remains insecure and scanty, and we are still dealing with a large number of unknown factors in this field.

There exists a considerable gap in our capacity to predict with any degree of certainty. We have no way of foretelling, when we look at a three-year-old child with certain tendencies towards anxiety or even symptom formation, whether and in what direction these tendencies will develop. We are equally uncertain about the clinical pictures that are likely to emerge and succeed each other in any child patient, or what effect, exactly, certain external conditions that we know to be unfavourable for mental health will give rise to in any given child. The great variety of factors, internal and external, which act upon each other, and their inter-relations, are as yet explored only insufficiently. Even in gross traumatic situations we do not know which element of the situation will have an immediate effect and what the inner condition of the given moment will select as the most operative element of the external one. An illuminating example of this is to be found in the case published by Mary Bergen (1958), a former student of the Hampstead Child-Therapy Course, on a child who was present when her father murdered her mother.

This introduction may sound discouraging, but its aim is to encourage thoughts into all areas in which we are eager to know more. It should make us aware of the need for our participation in research material even if it seems unlikely at first sight that it has played an important part in the subsequent disturbances.

I have the good fortune to be on the staff of a clinic in which a spirit of enquiry and the wish to learn form the centre of all work.

It will be my aim to give you a picture of the research work that is being carried out at this clinic. While trying to acquaint you briefly with some of the studies, their aims, techniques and first findings, I shall be touching on general problems of research that are encountered by those who base their investigations on material from individual psychotherapy and psychoanalysis.

The clinic I have referred to is the Hampstead Child-Therapy Clinic in London, which is directed by Miss Anna Freud. This Clinic differs from other clinics in London mainly in two ways:

1. all staff, psychiatrists, psychologists, child psychotherapists and psychiatric social workers are psychoanalytically trained;
2. the Clinic is financed by a number of foundations in the United States and is therefore independent of the local authority, although it is serving the community in the district in which it is situated. The funds supplied from the respective foundations are given with the express purpose of providing psychoanalytical treatment and research based on it. The research work I shall be describing is therefore entirely based on the principles and technique of Freudian psychoanalysis.

The need for planned research in psychoanalysis has long been felt. Workers in allied fields—psychiatrists, psychologists and sociologists—have often accused psychoanalysts of being unscientific in their thinking and of basing their work on hypotheses, which they were reluctant to prove.

There exist a number of reasons that make it clear why psychoanalysts are faced with specific problems when dealing with planned research. It may be of value to be aware of these before dealing with single projects.

The first and, to my mind, most important factor lies in the psychoanalytic method itself, as it was devised by Freud and has continued to develop both as a therapeutic method and as a method of investigation of the human mind. It is a long-term process, which takes place within the relationship of the patient to his analyst; it is in this relationship that the patient expresses his thoughts, experiences feelings, recalls and re-lives memories. Gradually he gains a new awareness of his inner and outer world, which enables him to deal with his conflicts and anxieties in a new way that is more adapted to the reality of the world he lives in.

Although you are probably familiar with the central role of the patient–doctor relationship, I have briefly recalled it at this point, as it contains most of the elements that seem to me to be essential for the correct and full understanding of the problems arising from it for all research that is based on material gained from psychotherapeutic work with individual patients. If we set out to investigate a process of a dynamic nature that takes place between two human beings, we must be aware of the fact that demands we may feel justified to make in other fields of research with regard to exactness and reliability cannot be applied here.

Proof by validation and quantification, which is a prerequisite for research in experimental psychology, psychoanalysis has to do without. We have no experimental situation that can be repeated exactly. Each therapeutic session is unique.

Attempts must therefore be made to counteract the subjectivity and other sources of error that arise from the fact that the analyst is alone with his patient. Recording machines have been introduced, observers placed behind one-way screens by those who were eager to do away with inexact methods. We must recognize, however, that by attempting to use these for the purpose of verification, we no longer investigate precisely what we have set out to study. Although some research workers assure us that it makes no difference to the patient or to themselves whether they are observed or listened to, an alien factor is introduced into the setting. What appears as a gain in accuracy may turn out to be a loss of far greater importance if it interferes with the freedom of expression of both partners in the therapeutic process.

The consulting room is the psychoanalyst's laboratory. We have to accept the shortcomings that result from this and have to plan our research techniques accordingly. There are, however, some factors that may compensate for these shortcomings. As Susan Isaacs (1939) has expressed it: 'In psychoanalytic research intensity of examination replaces extensity of sampling'.

Another problem lies in the small number of patients with the same psychopathology that any one analyst can treat. To remedy this, the method of 'pooling' has been devised, in which a number of analysts bring together their material. The danger of subjectivity is at the same time counteracted by careful record writing, reporting and detailed discussion with all other members of the research team. Work of this kind has become possible only since psychoanalytic work or psychotherapy based on these principles has spread out from the private consulting rooms where it was first practised, to the large number of clinics where it is in use now and, consequently, larger numbers of cases have become available.

We can now turn to the next question and ask: 'Who are the research workers in the field, and what specific qualifications do they need?'

I should like to answer this question in Dr Marjorie Brierley's (1951) words, quoting from her book: *Trends in Psycho-Analysis,* where she says:

> Every psychoanalyst should regard it as part of his professional duties to do what he can in the matter of verifying accepted hypotheses and testing new ones in the light of his experiences in his daily work. The same appies to the child guidance worker, if he is aware of the link between the work he does in practice and the theory on which its foundation rests.
>
> Theory is, in essence, simply intelligent explanation; an explanation based upon adequate evidence, which indicates the relationships existing among the data it covers.

I think it is true to say that awareness and clarity of theory and its link with practical therapeutic work is not always clearly formulated in the minds of those who carry out therapeutic work, and, although we know that sensitivity and intuition have an important place in this work, the absence of theoretical thinking is certainly a serious disadvantage, both to clinical and research work.

The urgency of keeping pace with their day-to-day work has led many child guidance workers over the years to pay less attention to the relationship that exists between clinical work and theory than is needed for favourable progress in both. It has led many to accept unquestioningly, certain findings put forward as hypotheses by others in the field. Such acceptance without continuous regard to the context in which the ideas have arisen leads to misconceptions; generalization and simplification of ideas that are meaningful and valuable make them deceptive and eventually create problems both for therapy and research.

Discussing this problem in a paper entitled 'The Child Guidance Clinic as a centre of prophylaxis and enlightenment', Anna Freud (1960b) says:

> The usefulness of any one clinic stands in direct proportion to the extent of knowledge on which practical work is based. Any body of Child Guidance workers has a double duty: on the one hand to apply existing knowledge to the practical work with children, on the other hand to work constantly towards an increase of knowledge by investigating problems, which have been insufficiently studied so far. Thus it is the double aim of application of facts and further fact finding that underlies the range of the clinic's activities.

It is clearly a matter of specific gift, interest and training that determines the part any analyst or therapist or any member of a clinic will want to and be able to play in its research work. A closer look at what is covered by the term 'research' in a child guidance clinic may help us to get a more concrete picture at once. If we make a first division into: (a) discovery of new facts and formulation of new hypotheses, and (b) verification of existing facts, we shall agree that while those who can contribute to the first group—finding new facts and making links so far not made—are relatively few and equipped with special creative powers, those among ourselves and our co-workers in a position to take an active part in the work of clarification and verification of existing hypotheses are potentially very large; in fact, every clinic worker could have a part in this work.

The nature and variety of research projects any given clinic will want to and be in a position to work on depends to a large extent on the specific aspects of problems any one member may be sufficiently interested in, so as to win other members of the staff to join him in this project. It will also depend on the nature of cases the given clinic tends to get, according to the district in which it finds itself and according to its relationship with various referring agencies.

I shall now briefly acquaint you with a number of research projects in process of investigation at our Clinic, adding to each the aim and the technique used in carrying it out.

The investigation of pathological states themselves

An inquiry into the analysis of psychotic–borderline cases

The aim of this study is to provide material for improved diagnosis between neurotic borderline cases, and special emphasis is given to (a) the use of language and its distortion, (b) the acting out of primitive impulses versus verbalization, (c) the profusion and eruption of phantasy life and its defensive use against anxiety stemming from external reality, (d) detailed comparison of reality-adapted functioning with normal and neurotic children, and (e) the nature of the child's ties to members of his family and his relation to himself and to lifeless objects.

For the purpose of this and similar studies, members of staff who are dealing with a case belonging in this category are invited to 'pool' their material with all others who treat similar cases. For this purpose they have to agree to:

1. keep detailed records, write a weekly report and make it available to the co-ordinator of the project and any other member of the research team;

2. take part in a weekly meeting at which specific questions are discussed, items in different cases compared, literature consulted and compared;

3. write full bi-monthly and six-monthly reports to make comparison possible;

4. make an abstract of all relevant items in the case material for the purpose of indexing, thereby making comparison of finer details possible.

External circumstances

Another type of project lays more stress on the relation of external circumstances to the child's disturbance. In this group I include the studies of the parents' and siblings' impact on the developing child. One of the projects belonging here is the one based on the material gained in *concurrent analyses of mothers and children,* about which I shall give a more detailed account later. Also, the analytic investigation of identical twins and their problems forms part of this category.

As I said before, we are not in a position to devise experiments so as to expose our children to the same situations, as is done in experimental psychology. We can, however, replace this to some extent by studying children for whom similar experiences have been 'devised by fate itself'. I am here referring to children who, for example, experienced separations, hospitalization, the loss of parents, have been adopted, lived in concentration camps, etc. As long as we remain aware that these apparently identical external circumstances represent only one aspect of a total dynamic constellation, in which preceding experiences, subsequent and present relationships and the coincidence with the child's thoughts and phantasies create a unique situation for each child, we may safely enter into research on the effect of the external event on his subsequent disturbance.

Physical handicaps

A third group centres on the effect of the child born with a *physical handicap,* centring so far on children born blind.

Child development

There is the wide field for research into problems of child development itself. A study of adolescents, for instance, in which we aim at clarifying problems arising from the process of maturation itself and its repercussions on the emotional state, simultaneously improves techniques of treatment for this specially difficult age group that tends to resist psychotherapy.

Longitudinal observations

We are in a position to combine longitudinal observations with subsequent analytic study in a number of children at present in their late adolescence whom we knew and observed in our daily lives with them in our residential war nursery as babies and through their first years. Here we compare our early observations with subsequent material from psychoanalysis and gain insight into questions of importance, namely whether, and how, certain trends that appeared to us, as outside observers, relevant in their early childhood, have continued to develop subsequently.

Research into simultaneous treatment
of mother and child

I shall now turn, in more detail, to the project of the pathogenic effect of neurotic mothers on their growing children
and to our study of the material of mother–child couples in
simultaneous treatment. In the last two decades the effect of
what is often referred to as the mother's rejection of the child
has come into the centre of attention. As with many new
hypotheses, this was widely taken up and widely applied.
Study of the first contacts the infant makes with his environment and of his first emotional responses to it has focussed
our attention on the fundamental importance of the mother
and her attitude to the child from the very beginning. With
the growing knowledge of the emotional needs of children in
the earliest phase, those mothers who fail to provide for
them—or for some of them—have been made responsible for
a large variety of childhood disturbances, psychoses and
psychosomatic disturbances, and the literature on this subject is very extensive.

There is no doubt that there are mothers who reject their
child and who are totally unwilling to bring it up, but it is of
greater importance to distinguish between this relatively
small group of truly rejecting mothers and the manifold
experiences of rejection undergone by children whose mothers by no means belong to this group.

In her paper on the subject, Anna Freud (1960a) distinguished between the internal and external factors by
which the mother–child unit can be affected in such a way
that the feeling of being rejected by the mother is experienced by the child, while it is incorrect and unhelpful dia-
gnostically and therapeutically to deal with the mother as a
'rejecting mother'.

In studying these children, and by investigating their
mothers' pathology as well as the external conditions, it has
been found that the absence or loss of favourable emotional
contact with the mother, which is so often covered by the

term 'rejection', contains a wide variety of factors. The following are only a few of these factors, in addition to the mother's real unwillingness to have a child and to care for it.

Experiences of rejection
through the mother's abnormality

(1) Much research has been done and many publications deal with the problem of the effect on the child of the mother's incapacity to establish a consistent relationship with him owing to psychotic elements or to a circumscribed psychosis. The mother's withdrawn state, her inability to make or maintain contact, to sense the child's needs and respond to them, can be experienced by children as rejection by their mother.

(2) External circumstances, such as prolonged separation, mother's hospitalization etc., have a similar effect on the young child, unable to understand and differentiate between one or the other cause for loss of the mother's presence and emotional response.

(3) Furthermore, it seems of great importance to get detailed evidence on the fact that mothers can be well able to supply the child with what he needs at one stage and quite unable to tolerate manifestations of a later stage for reasons of their own psychopathology. A mother may delight in her small and helpless baby, enjoy feeding it and caring for it, but become anxious, angry and aggressive as soon as he gains physical independence, walks away from her or resists being trained for cleanliness. Or, conversely, we have encountered mothers who cannot hold or touch their small babies, as they feel the impulse to harm them, but whose phantasies do not interfere, to the same extent, once the child gets physically independent.

Examples chosen from this one brief investigation show the need to discriminate between objective factors of external reality and those felt by the child as real through misconception and because they have become distorted and enlarged in his phantasy. The differentiation between reality and phantasy concerning the mother, between wilful neglect and her withdrawal from the child at moments when she is depressed or when she is under the domination of a fear of harming it, are only a few examples of factors that had led to the conviction that by detailed and intensive investigation of both mothers and children we can gain insight that is valuable and applicable to our work with those where we are unable to do more than to see them at widely spaced intervals for a short time and where we rely on guesswork to a large extent.

The complicated interaction between mother and child, which is frequently dealt with in a summary fashion—referred to, for instance, as good or bad mother–child relationship—has seemed to us in need of detailed investigation. By analysing both mother and child and studying the material in detail, we hope to contribute to the existing understanding of the interaction between them. Through insight gained from intensive treatment, we learn to respect the depth in which certain aspects of this relationship are rooted and the extent of their ramifications. We may thus learn to evaluate with more certainty what we can hope to achieve by the various techniques available to us in the framework of the child guidance clinics.

Simultaneous treatment of mother and child

Aims of study

(1) *The therapeutic aim*

It is a well-known fact encountered by many psychotherapists that the mother's participation in her child's neurotic illness can be a serious obstacle to his recovery. This problem was first discussed 25 years go in a paper entitled 'Child analysis and the mother', by Dorothy Burlingham (1935b). She shows the manifold ways in which the changes brought about in the child through therapy can become intolerable to the mother. We meet this situation, for example, when a formerly passive, submissive and dependent boy becomes active, masculine and independent, or when a child who has shared the mother's hypochondriacal fears becomes freed from them and she thereby experiences an intolerable increase of anxiety, continually threatening his new-found stability and attempting to hold him back in the common bond their shared anxieties had produced.

In certain cases, where the child's and mother's neuroses are so intimately linked that the child's normal development to adulthood is threatened or where a threat of a mother's depressive breakdown is likely to result from an adolescent's successful turn towards independence from her, therapeutic intervention for both simultaneously is necessary. It is, of course, clear that it is only rarely possible to get intensive psychoanalytic treatment for both of them.

The selection of cases for this study has been indicated by these brief remarks. While scientifically every case would be of interest for the study of interaction between mother and child, practical limits dictated by time and financial considerations keep the number small. The mother and child couples in treatment at the Clinic so far were chosen among those where treatment of the child alone, and non-intensive work with the mother, had clearly indicated the degree of her involvement in the child's illness, and where prolonged work in one or more clinics had given unsatisfactory results, leading psychiatrists concerned to refer them for intensive treatment to the Hampstead Clinic.

In this group we find children with the severest form of school phobia, which basically rests on their incapacity to leave their mothers. Treatment reveals that anxieties concerning their mother's safety, phantasies that she might die or otherwise disappear in their absence, are powerful agents

in these cases, but that these fears are constantly reinforced by the mothers themselves through their own
doublefold feelings concerning the child's safety, and their
alternating from intense hostility to over-anxious protec-
tion. There are also cases where the demarcation line
between a mother's normal anxiety about her child's health
is transgressed and the mother's own hypochondria is
extended on to the child's body. These are mother–child
couples well-known to paediatricians, as they make the
round of their departments. The doctor's assurance that her
child is not suffering from any serious complaint is received
with disbelief and disappointment by these mothers, and
they seek a further examination in another paediatric hospital, until they are finally referred to the child guidance
clinic.

These may serve as examples of pictures presented by
some cases selected for simultaneous treatment. While many
who respond to a similar description are constantly successfully dealt with by psychiatrists and psychiatric social
workers, alteration of deeply anchored disturbances in the
mother cannot be reached without intensive treatment in
others.

(2) *The theoretical aims*

Some of the questions we had in mind when entering into
this research project can be formulated as follows:

1. What factors exist in the mother that we would con-
    sider to have had a pathogenic effect on the child in the
    various phases of his development?

2. Which of these are still likely to act adversely on the
    child at the present time?

3. Can we trace in what way different factors of a patho-
    genic nature reach the child and how they affect it?

4. Can we single out those pathogenic influences that
    make it clear to us why in these cases treatment of the
    child without concurrent treatment of the mother
    gives unsatisfactory results?

While the research centres on the problems of pathogenic effect, we hoped to learn something equally about the interaction between both partners where favourable elements are concerned.

Method

For each mother-and-child couple studied, a team of three analysts is needed: one each for the treatment of the mother and the child, and a third, referred to as the co-ordinator, to whom the other two report the material in detail.

Another investigator in the United States has carried out all three roles herself. The disadvantages for both therapy and reliability of findings seem, however, outweighed by the advantages of time saving and first-hand knowledge of both patients.

Fathers are seen in accordance with our practice in other cases. This means, whenever possible, before starting treatment and subsequently whenever a father asks for an interview or the therapist decides that this would be beneficial for the progress of the treatment.

First conclusions

While it is too soon to draw general conclusions, a number of observations that indicate the directions in which the usefulness of findings will lie have been made:

(1) As was first shown by Dorothy Burlingham (Burlingham, Goldberger & Lussier, 1955) in a case of simultaneous analysis and confirmed by cases studied since, there is a distinct difference in the pathogenic effect of the mother according to whether her neurotic conflicts relating to the child remain in the realm of her phantasy and she is able to refrain from making the child participate in them physically, or whether, on the contrary, the mother has to act under the domination of her impulses, and these actions involve the

child physically. In these cases, the hope of bringing about a far-reaching favourable change in the child without the mother being treated too is small. Cases of mothers' continued interest and participation in matters concerning the child's digestive process, handling of the child's body throughout his childhood, as for instance in one case where the mother insisted on pushing back his foreskin daily in the service of hygiene, stimulation through rhythmical stroking at bedtime extended long after the bedtime problem had disappeared, and a case in which actual sexual seduction had taken place have been studied. Such actions do not usually become known to us in superficial contacts with the mother, nor even in intensive treatment for a long time. Our material indicates that children who are tied to their mothers through continued physical experiences give away this fact in treatment only with great difficulty. The simultaneous fear of losing the satisfaction they gain, as well as the fear of their mother's reaction to having been given away are powerful enough to make children withhold such secrets. Only once the mother herself has been helped to deal with the problem, of which she feels guilty but unable to deal with without treatment, have we seen changes occur in the child as well as the mother.

We hope, however, that close study of the diagnostic material of these cases in which subsequently these conditions were revealed will lead us to detect their existence also where intensive treatment is not available, as it seems likely that certain items that have so far escaped our notice are observable early on, once we have learned to recognize them.

A mother's and her child's prolonged involvement in physical contact threaten the child's capacity to develop favourably in those respects that are found to be basic for normal emotional and sexual functioning of the adult. Features we encounter and study in these cases contain a number of elements well known to us from treatment of adults where so far we had material available only from the patient in retrospect and not from his mother (for example, certain cases of impotence or homosexuality).

The advantage for clearer differential diagnosis

A case in which a boy presented intense fears of being poisoned by bad food was especially enlightening (see chapters 5 and 6). While his misconceptions and his own phantasies leading to this fear could be singled out, ideas of a paranoid nature relating to the mother continued to present a serious picture as long as only the boy's material was taken into account; from the mother's analysis, however, it emerged that she was, in fact, dominated by phantasies of poisoning this child and that—although these phantasies were counteracted by extreme concern and care about his food—he was aware of her struggle against her impulses to harm him and reacted with a fear that had an element of reality; thereby the evaluation of the paranoid nature of his ideas was corrected and they eventually subsided.

Revaluation of a diagnosis, as a result of the mother's need to keep the child stupid or through common use of a schizophrenic-like language, has also been encountered.

Not only for the understanding of the effect of gross disturbances in the mother, but for the clarification of less severe manifestations does concurrent treatment serve a useful purpose.

Simultaneous analysis can also elucidate some of the concepts with which we are used to dealing continually in a global way. I should like to take the factor of the mother's inconsistency as an example. This is generally recognized as having a detrimental effect on the child's character development.

Inconsistency in her feelings about her child and the consequent handling can be seen to be built on two sources mainly—the one anchored in the mother's own character formation, by which we mean the result of the external influences in her early life, and the specific solutions of these, found in her internal conflicts between impulse and defensive forces in her—for example, the way in which she has dealt with her own aggressive impulses and consequently her reaction to the sight and experiences of other people's and specifically her own child's aggressive behaviour.

In this same category we may find a mother's lenient permissive attitude to a child's demandingness for food, her sudden violent turn against him when he arouses her disgust and a free or even seductive attitude to his demands for bodily contact. Through simultaneous analytic work, we learn to see the roots of these inconsistent and confusing changes of handling the child and their effects. Further study can teach us which of these attitudes we are likely to be able to influence through infrequent and non-intensive interventions and which we have to recognize as unalterable by these means. In child guidance, much of the work with parents is geared towards attempting to alter their reactions to the child, and much work is often built on trial and error plus intuition. This seems not only a disappointing approach, but also one that contains potential danger. It is well known, for instance, that mothers who have obsessional features influence their children's normal development adversely. Either attempts to draw their attention to the undesirability and adverse effect of their actions or immediate attempts to get at the basic meaning of the compulsive act can lead to severe anxiety and even a breakthrough of psychotic elements, unless one is fully aware of the defensive nature and function of the symptom and has gained respect for the fact that deep personality changes cannot be brought about without careful and prolonged work.

The second group of factors from which inconsistency has been found to stem is built on the mother's emotional experiences relating to people in her childhood or her present life. We have found that reactions to the child may alter in quick succession according to whether, at the given moment, he may have unwittingly evoked in her a feeling originally relating to a hated sister or brother, or a feature of her despised husband. Pride may be aroused about different aspects of the child's personality and achievements reminding the mother of her beloved father. To the child this changing inconsistent response is inexplicable, and analysis shows that he is not only hampered in unifying his feelings of loving and hating and his picture of the mother as a safe or dangerous person, but that his own capacity of becoming a unified being can be severely held up, or made impossible, where he is exposed to severe influences of the kind described. Again, we can learn from even a small number of such detailed studies to differentiate between those factors with which we can safely deal and certain others that, even though they might have become apparent to us as experienced workers early on in our talks with a parent, we must refrain from entering into, because we know that we cannot hope to alter them and may, by touching on them, adversely influence the internal equilibrium.

Our study suggests that we should not expect all children to show direct reactions to their mother's symptoms but that some of them are affected indirectly only. The mother's illness may interfere with her capacity for effective mothering generally, and in these cases the resultant disturbances of the children can be of a completely different nature from those of their mothers. It is far too simple and proves incorrect to follow the thesis that the child's neurosis is the direct result of the father's or mother's neurosis. The effect of a mother's depression by no means tells us that this child will be depressed. We hope, in time, to become better able to distinguish between the effect of the external agent and the result it produces within the child.

I have given much time to the research project on mother and child, and there is less opportunity of going into details about the project on the treatment of patients in puberty and adolescence. There are two reasons for this.

I decided to use the first project not only to describe it as such, but also in order to acquaint you with the lines of thought underlying our research work generally, and these apply equally to the adolescent project. Furthermore, there exists an overlap of both projects in an important section of our study of adolescents, because the mother–child project contains cases who entered treatment in puberty and who have become adolescents in the course of the investigation. In these cases we are studying the adolescent's failure to detach himself from his infantile ties and his reactions to the emotional and physical changes occurring in him, while simultaneously we have the opportunity of following the conflicts aroused in the mothers who have to face these changes in their children. The anxieties aroused in them and the consequent problems arising for the adolescent are of the greatest interest.

This, however, is only one section of the research project on adolescence, which has a wider aim. It is the experience of most people dealing with adolescents and pre-adolescents in psychotherapy that this work presents specific problems, whatever the nature of the psychotherapeutic intervention may be. A considerable number of adolescent disturbances indicate, however, that they are in need of psychotherapeutic intervention, often of an immediate nature, where a clinical picture presents itself or behaviour changes occur that are as disquieting to the adolescent as to his environment. Much has been written on the technical problems of getting an adolescent to come to treatment at all, from the fact that he resents any part played by the parents in relation to the child guidance clinic and from his attitude to the relationship with the therapist.

In this study, in which 20 analysts participate in studying 20 cases at present in treatment, we hope by pooling of detailed experiences to enter into the wide range of problems arising from the adolescent process itself and to adapt variations and changes of technique to its most typical features.

The sections at present being studied refer to the technical aspects of:

diagnosis and introduction to treatment;

the adolescent's capacity for insight into his need for treatment;

the therapeutic relationship and the problem it presents for the adolescent patient;

the adolescent's secretiveness and suspiciousness;

his reactions to his physical changes, and to his changing role in relation to his environment.

New sections for study are added as the cases present them and the method of pooling gives the opportunity for comparison and discussion.

I hope to have given you a picture of the research activities at the Hampstead Clinic, as well as our methods of work. The number of children we can study is small; what we find, we cannot express in statistics. Most projects are still in the state referred to by Dr Buckle, when one has to say: 'It is too soon to show results, we shall tell you something in a few years'. However, the Clinic's research workers have been and are publishing, whenever they feel that they have something worthwhile to say. These papers are to be found in the annual volumes of *The Psycho-Analytic Study of the Child*, published by International Universities Press of New York, and the Imago Publishing Company, London.

However small the contributions may seem in the vast field of child guidance, we hope that they will prove to have been of value.

CHAPTER ELEVEN

The ego's participation in the therapeutic alliance

with Liselotte Frankl

C ertain aspects of the problem of the ego's participation in the therapeutic alliance have recently been
discussed in regard to adult patients at a panel of the
American Psychoanalytic Association on 'Criteria for ana-
lyzability' (1960). On this occasion Elizabeth Zetzel discussed the criteria integral to the analytic situation: the
motivation for more than symptomatic relief, the capacity to
tolerate anxiety and frustration, the ability to maintain a
stable relationship and to sustain secondary-process thinking. All these enable the patient to remain in the analytic
situation despite the anxieties experienced in the transference neurosis. For a successful analysis the patient must

Read at the 22nd International Psycho-Analytical Congress, Edin-
burgh, July–August, 1961, and reprinted from *The International Journal of Psycho-Analysis* (1962), 43 (4, 5): 333–337.

be able to maintain some mature ego attributes in the analytic situation in spite of anxieties engendered by the analytic process. Also, the patient requires sufficient flexibility to mobilize unresolved conflicts in a regressive transference neurosis. Loewenstein (1954) has contributed several valuable papers to the problem of the therapeutic alliance.

It seemed important to us to study the therapeutic alliance in child patients, as it manifests itself in the treatment of children of various ages. Closer scrutiny of the various aspects of ego development and the part they play in promoting or hindering our therapeutic endeavours is needed. This can further elucidate certain difficulties in the treatment of adult patients, which arise from arrest of certain aspects of ego development, from regression, or from certain ego defects.

Analytic work is based on our access to and understanding of the unconscious content, and the communications reaching us through transference. The therapeutic process rests on the communications we make to the patient of what we have understood and felt about his inner world. The communication we have chosen to make is in the first place made to his ego, and it is *via* the ego that communication becomes effective. It is, therefore, essential for favourable progress in treatment to be aware of the important role the ego plays in transmitting to and assimilating into the personality the analyst's communications.

The analyst who is aware of this considers it his task to evaluate carefully the ego's relations both to the inner and outer world. Problems of choice of interpretations, including what Freud referred to as tact, as well as timing and formulation, must play a constant part in the analyst's thinking. One of the considerations in making this choice is determined by our evaluation and anticipation of the child's capacity to take in and assimilate what we are communicating to him at any given time. Our own way of conveying to the child that we keep in touch with his feelings of the moment, for example his anxiety or sadness and the relief he experiences through this, paves the way for a relationship that gradually enables him to feel that he wants to share with his analyst more of his phantasy life, as well as his day-to-day experiences.

Experience of the analyst's empathy and the feeling that the analyst understands the child's need to defend himself further helps the child to develop this relationship. On this basis he can stand up to the first experiences of having to face anxiety and guilt, resulting from defence interpretations, as well as phases, even of intense resistance and negative transference. By conveying to the child that we are in touch with his rapidly changing feelings, and essentially through verbalization, we simultaneously help the self-observing function of the child's ego to become operative and gradually to become the valuable ally needed for successful analytic work.

It is, however, not only essential to be in touch with the child's phantasies and feelings and to put them into words. In doing so we must remain aware of the ego's changing capacity to make use of words and keep in touch with the nature of the child's thought processes as they develop. In work with very young patients, of 2–2½ years, it is especially important to realize that causal thinking develops only slowly. The formulation of complicated interpretations which rest on the understanding of causality can therefore obviously not be made full use of.

Though awareness of the developmental level reached by the young child appears to be a basic requirement of which every analyst is aware, we find in practice that children's capacities to take in and assimilate interpretations tend to be overrated. They may, therefore, be faced with formulations well beyond their grasp through the use of concepts and abstract thinking that are not meaningful to them yet and tend to add to the child's confusion and his misconceptions. The differentiation between the child who has not yet reached the state when he is able to make the specific causal links and the blocking of this capacity depends on our intimate knowledge of details of the development of this ego function.

This approach, based on developmental factors, is not equally taken into consideration where the analyst makes contact with the child patient by directly confronting him with ego-alien id-contents. Such an approach contains serious dangers: immediate confrontation, which largely by-passes the defensive organization of the ego, may result in panic-like reactions and make the analyst into a magic person. The child's initial phantasies about the analyst's magic and omnipotent qualities are thereby confirmed. In this way the analyst counteracts rather than facilitates the child's capacity to feel that, alongside his projected phantasies, there exists a person whose aim it is to help him to differentiate between phantasy and reality within and outside himself.

A further reason why it is essential to keep in touch with the patient's ego lies in the fact that direct confrontation with the unconscious impulses rather than with their derivatives, which are closer to consciousness, may have an immediate seductive effect. Especially in the young patient who offers us access to his unconscious comparatively easily the temptation to take a line of direct approach is great. Through this he is easily precipitated into anxiety outbursts that make him flee the threatening interpretations or driven into defensive measures more intense than those established in him before entering treatment.

The developmental trend of latency to ward off the intensity of earlier oedipal and pre-oedipal wishes and the conflicts arising from them is reached by the strengthening of the ego's defensive measures. Analytic work can consequently be experienced as a threat to the equilibrium that is in the process of becoming established. Another important tendency in latency, however, leads to establishing the link with external reality more firmly. For this reason the child can accept the analyst's role as a representative of reality and as an ally on the way to clearer distinction between reality and phantasy, between contradictory feelings, opposing forces and his inner and outer world. As Elisabeth Geleerd (1957) has made clear, one aspect of the analyst's role is always that of representative of reality. Awareness of this aspect is a basic requirement for successful analytic work, even though it may become submerged temporarily during certain phases of treatment. The latency child's growing need to differentiate between phantasy and reality makes him wish to use the analyst also in his capacity to bring this clarification, and this contributes to the bond which helps him through stressful phases of his treatment.

Specific problems shown by latency children in the course of analytic treatment have been fully discussed by Bertha Bornstein. In her paper 'On latency' (1951), as in her contribution to the Panel on 'Technique related to development' (Bornstein, Falstein & Rank, 1951), she has drawn attention to the obstacles to treatment that arise from the trends inherent in the development during this phase. We have found these confirmed in those of our cases of school age in whom age-adequate developmental features were already present initially, while it was of great interest to meet with these typical resistances to treatment only late in the analysis of those children whose development had been arrested and who reached an age-adequate stage only as the result of the analytic work that had preceded it. Although latency children bring to treatment certain features that permit them to form a treatment alliance, we also meet with cases in this age group who show no wish to enter into contact with the analyst. From these we learn how, step by step, a careful approach via affect and defence interpretation can open up the capacity to establish a relationship, to communicate and finally to take part actively in the analytic work.

If we meet a patient in this age group who shows no signs of a wish to make contact or to communicate anything about himself and certainly no wish for help, various ways of approach can be chosen. The initial aim is common to all— namely, to reduce anxiety sufficiently to allow the child to enter into a relationship and make use of the analyst for therapeutic purposes. Close observation of behaviour and of non-verbal communications, knowledge of details of present and past circumstances and the consistent support of at least one of the parents can lead to establishing a therapeutic relationship purely on the basis of interpretative work also in children who initially meet us with violent hostility.

In the case of a girl of ten years, initially brought against her will, it was possible to follow in detail the steps that led to a 'treatment alliance' and to a favourable result followed up into adult life.

Following a prolonged separation from her mother at 18 months, Angela's personality had shown a marked change after the mother's return. Intense pleasure in inflicting pain on her mother had soon spread to tormenting animals and later her baby brother, who was born when she was six years old. She seemed compelled to make sudden sadistic attacks, and her excitement and pleasure while inflicting pain were freely shown. The absence of manifest guilt and of the wish to make good what she had done made it extremely difficult for adults around her to deal with her sympathetically. Both her parents, but especially her father, had break-throughs of violent temper; the marriage had brought constant quarrels, which the child had witnessed. Later her sadism had turned against the baby brother, but her pleasure in tormenting animals had started long before and remained unchanged after his birth. At the age of ten her cruelty seemed at times to reach dangerous proportions: animals and small children had escaped serious harm repeatedly only by some chance intervention of an adult. Open hostility to her father and a serious learning inhibition, which hindered normal school progress in spite of an IQ of 167, had convinced the mother of the need for analytic treatment, while the father remained doubtful.

Angela treated the analyst as a dangerous enemy from the moment she saw her and concentrated on her all her hate and aggression. She refused to enter the room and to take off her hat and coat, and she did not talk. She kept an eye on every one of her analyst's movements with a tense expression and a panic-like state, ready to escape or to attack. She did both in turn, sometimes running away after the first few minutes, sometimes approaching the analyst and suddenly attacking her by treading on her foot or pinching her from the back. Her first words were swear-words in response to the analyst's first communications. The latter were aimed at reducing the hostile attacks by showing Angela the defensive aspect from which their intensity derived. The analyst consistently interpreted her behaviour, as derived from her identification with a phantasied aggressor, and thereby brought about the first verbal communications, through which Angela revealed the content of her own sadistic phantasies and activities, which she had immediately projected onto the unknown analyst. Soon after, she revealed her fear of her father's violent outbursts. The first interpretations that had con-fronted her with the phantasied nature of the attacks she expected from the analyst led to the recognition of the two main sources of her approach to the analyst as to a danger-ous enemy, viz., the projection of her own sadistic wishes and the precursors of transference in which the danger situation made the analyst into the dangerous father at once.

The phase of direct bodily attack and verbal abuse was followed by a treatment phase in which she was tempted to force the analyst completely into her control, prescribing every gesture she was to make, every word to say, severely threatening her for any signs that she had a will or power of her own. Any unexpected movement or word brought a shocklike reaction, as if she were expecting to be hurt. In this way she made the analyst experience her own fears and simultaneously warded off her anxiety that arose from the projection of her own impulse to do harm. The analyst continued to deal consistently with the defensive measures, only confining herself to those areas where the affect was most immediate. She avoided entering into the content of the terrifying phantasies and their deeply unconscious meaning. This led step by step to the decrease of the projections that had made it impossible, at first, for

Angela to see or feel the reality of the analyst and her real intentions, alongside her phantasies. Angela came to understand her need to reverse the roles and to control every one of the analyst's movements. This began to open the way for her to test the analyst as a real object of trust, who remains unscathed and unaltered in spite of the manifold aspects transferred on her.

An extreme case of this kind is instructive from many points of view. With regard to our attempt to differentiate the therapeutic alliance from transference phenomena, we can see here that in the large majority of cases we do not experience negative transference as an obstacle that brings treatment to a prolonged standstill, because one element in the ego keeps touch with the reality of the analyst and his real role. Such loss of touch with reality or the incapacity to take in and react to real and good features of external objects is usually characteristic of psychotic patients. In certain cases of child patients and especially in adolescents it appears that the anxiety concerning the person and role of the analyst is enormously heightened temporarily through the coincidence of intense projection, a real frightening object in the family whose features are transferred to the analyst and the developmental stage of the object relationship, which makes the adult an intruder who has to be warded off.

In the case of Angela, as in others who resist treatment tenaciously, a great amount of work is needed to arrive at a point where the child is able to face the fact that the disturbance and suffering in his life are located within him and not in the external world only. Immediate relapse into attacking behaviour followed the analyst's first attempt at showing her that her communications about other people, especially about an abnormal child in the neighbourhood, contained aspects of herself. As long as they were not expressly related to her, she was able to take in the meaning of interpretations and to participate actively in the analysis by bringing further thoughts and feelings related to them. Again, the need to externalize, to displace, to split off certain intolerable aspects are well known to us in patients of all ages. The tenacious fight against the recognition of defences can create an obstacle in child treatment unless the analyst remains aware that what is needed is to refrain from making himself into a persecuting figure by dealing too rapidly with defence interpretation and especially with ego-alien content, without giving the patient time to make the process of assimilation at his own pace.

In Angela's treatment the awareness of her intolerance of facing her own cruelty and guilt brought a very productive phase in which the content of her most defended sadistic wishes was entirely dealt with through the neighbour's child, allowing her to express her feelings and phantasies *via* him without attempting to interpret the displacement. She actively began to look for unconscious motivations in others whose behaviour she disapproved of—for instance she said 'Jeremy was so cruel to a bird today, do you think he was afraid of something?' Here she turns to the analyst for help for the first time, links the cruelty to fear, and through her question tells the analyst that she expects help from her to see the true link. Soon after this she can express disapproval, and later her guilt is expressed for the first time in another question to the analyst, inviting her to show disapproval of cruel impulses in the other child. The slow process leading from here to the point when she became able to face her own destructive wishes, the instinctual satisfaction she derived from them and the relation of these phantasies and actions to her masturbatory activities was made on the basis of her ever greater capacity to participate actively in the analysis. The self-observing function had gained strength and had led to active participation, especially when it became allied to the capacity to maintain an object relationship.

Simultaneously, during this early phase of treatment, the slow process with its carefully timed interpretations has gradually freed the child's capacity to feel and maintain the relationship to the real aspect of the analyst in her therapeutic function, alongside the intense feelings arising from the changing aspects experienced in the transference.

In Angela the phase of total distrust and expectation of hostility from the analyst was comparatively short. In her positive reactions to the interpretations of the defensive nature of her fears her basic experience of satisfactory mothering in the earliest phase of her life played an important part. In the course of her analysis it became evident that, in spite of the traumatic separation in the second year and the hate against her mother arising from this, the aspect of her mother as a loving and satisfying person who was able to sense her feelings and bring comfort was well established in her and could therefore come to play its part in the treatment. This found expression in her emerging positive transference feelings derived from the relationship to the mother and simultaneously in her capacity to trust the analyst's willingness and ability to help her. Through this she was able to become an active participant in her treatment.

In cases where the experience of good mothering has been severely interfered with from the start—for instance, by psychotic elements in the mother—the establishment of a treatment alliance with the analyst can only be the result of a far longer phase of work. Only after prolonged work is the child enabled to differentiate between his own feelings of love and hate and to react to the real positive and negative qualities he meets in other people. During this phase the projective aspects of the distrust have to be analysed, but even when these have been much diminished, the child has to test the reality of the analyst's trustworthiness again and again, because throughout his past life and in his current experience with his mother her real impulses and actions tend to confirm his phantasies. For example, in the case of a boy whose mother's destructive and seductive impulses led to severe impairment of her capacity to care for him adequately, especially in the earliest phase, his approach to the analyst was for a long time characterized by the almost complete absence of good expectations from her.

It is well known that the analyst faces a variety of problems when attempting to establish and maintain a treatment alliance with patients in puberty and throughout adolescence. These can be understood in terms of the developmental changes taking place in these phases. The coincidence of the changes within the structure of the personality with the intensification of id impulses and the simultaneous struggle for freedom from the tie to the infantile love objects creates a situation in which many elements contained in the analytic process and especially the tie to the analyst are felt as a threat.

Specific problems arising from these developmental factors are encountered at the initial stage with patients who have reached the phase in which one of the many forms of adolescent revolt have set in. Among patients in this age group who are referred for treatment, we meet with a considerable number who come for the very reason that their development has been held up. Analytic work here aims at freeing the forward movement, and only after successful treatment do we experience the typical obstacles to active participation in treatment with the repercussions in the transference of the adolescent's need to loosen the object tie.

Summary

While much thought has been given to problems of interpretation in the treatment of adult patients, they have, as yet, not been studied with all their implications where children are concerned. One aspect of importance is related to the changes taking place in the child's developing ego, the part of the personality to which interpretations are conveyed. It is clear that in the course of development questions relating, for instance, to the growing capacity to tolerate frustration or to master anxiety must affect the choice, formulations and timing of interpretations. It must be kept in mind that in many cases that are referred for treatment, different aspects of the ego are not on a level corresponding to the child's age. Attention is drawn to the need to remain aware of this in order to find the optimal conditions for transmission and assimilation of interpretations into the personality of child patients.

CHAPTER TWELVE

Some observations on mothers of children with intellectual inhibitions

The observations I shall be discussing have not been collected systematically with the intention of doing research on the subject. They have been gained, as we usually gain material in psychoanalytic work, from cases that have come to us by chance, at intervals of several years.

In recent years our interest is turning more and more towards the relation existing between the child's disturbance and certain features of the parents, especially the mother, by which the child has been affected from his earliest days onwards. Simultaneous analysis of mother and child is beginning to give us more detailed insight into the interplay between them. So far, unfortunately, it is rare to have the

Paper read at the General Meeting of the Hampstead Child Therapy Clinic on 8 April 1954. Reprinted from *Psychoanalytic Study of the Child* (1954), 9:259–273.

opportunity of working on analytic material of both mother and child.

No analytic material is available of the mothers I shall be describing. One of them has been in analysis for some time but broke it off, and her analyst, who has left the country, told me only a few details at the time. My direct knowledge of the mothers is confined to the talks I have had with them at varying intervals during their children's treatment in the course of two to three years. I have also used information gained from their husbands, where they were available, and of course from the children's analyses.

So far I have studied three cases in detail. A further case that I have supervised, namely the case I have published with Ivy Bennett (Bennett & Hellman, 1951), shows close similarities. Comparison of these cases, which present similar clinical pictures, show a number of striking similarities in the children's mothers.

I first want to give a brief description of the children. At the time when they came for treatment, Jimmy was eight years old, Nicky was eleven and Bettina twelve. The pictures presented by the three children I analysed (between 1947 and 1952) had the following features in common: intense separation anxiety when leaving mother, with consequent tearful scenes on going to school; inability to bear frustration, resulting in frequent crying and extensive use of auto-erotic satisfactions of an oral nature. Nicky and Jimmy sucked their thumbs as soon as they felt in the least anxious, and they did so for a great part of the day, especially at school. Bettina was compelled to carry a bag of sweets, from which she ate continuously when anxious and frustrated.

The main reason for seeking treatment was their failure to acquire knowledge of the basic school subjects. At the age of eleven, Nicky was unable to spell any three-letter word correctly; Jimmy, eight years old, could neither read nor write. Bettina's disturbance was the most severe. At the age of eleven, she presented a picture of pseudo imbecility, similar to the one described in Berta Bornstein's famous case (1930). Their memories were severely impaired, and their amnesia extended beyond normal age. They were physically clumsy and frequently ill. The boys had repeated minor accidents; Jimmy broke his arm, Nicky his arm and later his collar bone. In all cases lying was a prominent problem, much emphasized by the mothers.

Psychoanalysts have given much attention to the problem of intellectual inhibition, especially with regard to children, and the literature on the subject is extensive. We find the term 'intellectual inhibition' used in a twofold way, referring to inhibition of the *process* of intellectual development as a whole, as well as to inhibition of certain ego functions of intelligence. Where the inhibition of the *developmental process* is concerned, we usually speak of total intellectual inhibition, pseudo debility or pseudo imbecility. The inhibition of certain functions, or partial inhibition of intelligence, is well known to us as learning inhibitions in school children. They may range from lack of interest in certain subjects to a total incapacity to acquire knowledge and skill in one or several fields. In the first case the result of intelligence tests leaves us puzzled, because it is difficult to answer the question whether we are dealing with an innate poor endowment or with arrested development; in the other case, we find striking discrepancies between the functions that have been impaired and those that have developed unrestrictedly.

In *Inhibitions, Symptoms and Anxiety*, Freud (1926) states: 'An inhibition is the expression of a restriction of an Ego function. These restrictions have either been imposed as a measure of precaution or have been brought about as the result of an impoverishment of energy. The Ego renounces these functions in order to avoid coming into conflict with the Id.' The genesis of intellectual inhibition conforms to this definition.

The need for inhibition may arise when a function has either (1) taken on an unconscious libidinal significance; or (2) taken on an unconscious, aggressive, destructive meaning.

If we approach the problem from the angle of *the purpose* served by the stupidity resulting from the inhibition of intellectual functions, we frequently find that it originates in the need to display absence of knowledge about sexual matters in order to retain the parents' love. Stupidity may also stand for a display of castration, in order to escape fear of castration and loss of love. Avoidance of destructive activities and masochistic, self-punishing aspects are also well known to be found in the exhibition of 'not knowing'.

The role played by the disturbance of the child's early relation to the mother has been emphasized by many authors, who stress the great significance of oral fixation in cases of intellectual inhibition. The close, unconscious link between intake of knowledge and intake of food was first stressed by Abraham. In her paper on pseudo debility, Berta Bornstein (1930) has demonstrated clearly how great the influence of oral traumata was in the case of the girl she describes. While the role played by the mother is implied in these cases, the problem has not, so far, been approached from the angle of the mother's personality, except by Mahler (1942), who sees the child's stupidity linked with unconscious needs of both mother and child.

My own material contains ample confirmation of these main aspects and clearly illustrates Mahler's findings concerning the unusually intimate bond existing early between these patients and their mothers. There is, in addition, one feature in common to all the mothers I have observed, which plays an important part not only in understanding the children's need to inhibit intellectual functions but also in explaining the special bond between them and their mothers.

Though the mothers appeared to have little in common externally, certain important similarities can be found already in comparing the first interviews.

Jimmy's mother, a strikingly beautiful, tall, Scandinavian woman with artistic gifts, showed herself deeply concerned about his problem. She spent much time describing the link that existed between her and this child. She emphasized that Jimmy was so much closer to her than his older sister or younger brother. He was, from the very start, like a part of herself; and it was a deeply painful realization to find that she herself was now unable to help him. She quite openly showed her fear of losing this intimate contact, once I had intruded into their bonds. She then proceeded, with considerable dramatization, to make a confession: she said she felt it would be essential for my complete understanding of Jimmy's case to know that she had a lover. Although happily married to a man she loved, another man had meant complete happiness to her until recently. She described how he had enriched not only her own but also her husband's and the children's lives. Jimmy's attachment to this man had become so close that his recent departure had been felt by the boy as severely as by herself.

The outstanding features of this first interview with Jimmy's mother were found again in the first contacts with the mothers of the other children:

1. the description of the specially close bond between mother and child;
2. intense fear of losing this intimate relationship;
3. a confession, which is followed by a far-reaching denial of reality, emphasizing reversal of affects.

If we compare the content of the confessions, we find that Jimmy's mother confessed having had a lover until recently; Nicky's mother confessed having had a lover while her husband was away in the war and having subsequently married him.

If we compare the content of the denial, which followed the confession in each case, we find that Jimmy's mother denied that either her husband or the children had negative feelings towards the other man. She even emphasized their love for him and their sadness about his departure. Nicky's mother vividly described his lack of interest in and even hatred against his own father and emphasized his great love for the man who had become her second husband.

In Bettina's case the situation was somewhat different: nevertheless, we find the essential features again. Bettina's mother, too, described the close bond between herself and the child, not, however, as something she appreciated and enjoyed but as an intense irritation. The child, however stupid she may have appeared otherwise, seemed to sense her mother's feelings and disturbed her peace of mind through it. A constant cycle of scenes and reconciliations was played off between mother and daughter, reminding the mother of her relationship with her own mother. She then proceeded to confess that she had a lover and that she felt guilty about it. Her husband had remained in Central Europe and was sent to a concentration camp, and she did not know whether he was really dead. She assured me at once that Bettina no longer remembered her father and never referred to him. She was 4½ years old when she last saw him. Again we find the self-accusation on the one hand, the denial on the other.

All these mothers are compelled to deny reality in order to reduce their guilt. The children are therefore permitted to know reality and feel real feelings only in so far as this is tolerable to the mothers.

One might ask at this point what the function of these confessions may have been? Remembering Dorothy Burlingham's paper 'Compulsion to confess and need for punishment' (1935a), we know the function of the confession to be a twofold one: to form a close bond with the person to whom the confession is made—in our cases, with the analyst, against whom strong, negative feelings exist—and simultaneously to reduce guilt. Retrospectively it is possible to see that, indeed, both these components have played an important part. A third function of the confessions became clear only towards the end of each child's treatment, when it was found that the 'confession' had been hiding another secret. The initial confession thus served as a screen behind which another, more guilty secret was concealed. This secret, however, came to light only after the children's intellectual inhibitions had been removed to a large extent.

To return to the mothers: they can best be described as hysterical characters, displaying emotions freely, dramatizing and showing a tendency to untruthfulness. In two cases,

that of Nicky's and Bettina's mothers, we find a fully established anxiety hysteria with conversion symptoms and
pseudologia, for which Nicky's mother had sought treatment. The tendency to deny reality has been mentioned
before. Insight into the nature and extent of their lying
could, of course, only be detected very gradually, when
uncertainties, contradictions and the repetitive content of
certain falsifications of facts began to form a pattern.

All these mothers were uncertain about details of their
own past or refused to give details, pretending to have forgotten them, while they told and retold certain memories with
varying details and dramatizations. The leading theme in
all, however different the setting of their childhood had been,
was the father's ridigity and lack of response to the daughter's love, which had made their childhood miserable. They
had always been conscious of setting an example of high
moral standards to others. The suffering endured through
the father's strictness formed the ever recurring theme of
their memories. They described their relations with their
mothers as very close and loving. Jimmy's and Nicky's mothers had lost their own mothers during adolescence and were
expected to keep house afterwards. This had increased the
antagonism between themselves and their fathers.

All the children's mothers had left home between the ages
of 17 and 19 years; all had formed a pre-marital relationship
within one or two years of leaving home. They were ineffi-
cient housewives but entertaining and gifted in many ways
and most attractive to men.

They emphasized how happy they had been about the
birth of these babies and how the pregnancy and the child's
birth had been a most satisfying experience. The pleasure in
feeding and caring for babies was outstandingly marked in
all of them; the amount of kissing, the permissiveness about
sucking were conspicuous. Oral needs were not only satisfied
but stimulated and overgratified.

In spite of this, the children were quite suddenly weaned,
apparently for external reasons, before they were five
months old, and separation from the mother followed in the

cases of Nicky and Bettina. The mothers described the distress and feeling of loss after sudden weaning, which they experienced themselves and observed in their children. Food has remained a great pre-occupation for all of them; their love and anxiety are always expressed in terms of food.

This early change from intense satisfaction to sudden frustration repeated itself again and again in the children's later lives. Alternation of oversatisfaction and frustration is well known to be one of the causes of fixation, and, in its oral aspect, it forms an obstacle to normal processes of introjection in the early phase.

As mentioned before, all children showed marked oral character traits and disturbances of an oral nature: compulsive sucking, prolonged into pre-puberty; compulsive eating and, in one case, addiction to a certain kind of sweet. In the transference their greedy demandingness was characteristic, and fantasies of eating and biting and the fear of being bitten and swallowed were prominent. In critical phases of their lives each of the children had gone through eating difficulties, which had caused great anxiety to the mothers; threatening separations brought a refusal of food in the boys' cases as a means of keeping the mother with them. The link between the inhibition of their oral aggression and their inhibition of learning became clear when the analysis of this material brought marked improvement in their school progress.

I shall now turn to the other basic aspect of intellectual inhibition and discuss the observations relating to the fate of the child's curiosity and scopophilia. It is well known, and much discussed in earlier cases, that the rebuff experienced by the child in his early attempts to acquire sexual knowledge plays an important part in intellectual inhibitions. When the child's curiosity regarding the body and its functions, as well as his interest in his parents' sexual relations, meet with severe prohibitions, curiosity and learning may, in general, become dangerous and have to be given up or much restricted in order to retain the parents' love. Clandestine observations, arousing instinctual danger, have to be repressed, thus leading to impairment of memory and inhibition of looking.

In the cases observed, the inhibition of curiosity, and especially of looking, has a more complicated basis, which is to be found in certain disturbed traits of all these mothers. In all cases sexual information had been given early. In each case it was also found that the child had been given unusually great opportunities to see the mother's naked body. All children not only had free access to bathroom and toilet when the mother was there, but were frequently encouraged to be present when toilet and bath were used. The mother's bath time had been the centre of the intimate relationship with Jimmy, Nicky and Bettina. Although brothers and sisters, too, had free access to the bathroom, they were not specially encouraged to come and seemed to have accepted the fact that it was this *one* child's privilege.

Gradually it became evident that what they displayed to them was not only their feminine beauty and the pleasure derived from their body, but that at times the emphasis altered from this to the display of their defects and sufferings. Nicky's mother, who suffered from the fear of bleeding to death, never failed to let him know about her menstruation and, among other things, demonstrated her Caesarian scar to him. Jimmy's mother, who was so very beautiful but obsessed with the fear of getting fat, frequently mentioned that he was a better judge than any man could be regarding her figure, her clothes, her hair. Jimmy was always consulted, and she complained to him of any gain in weight. Bettina's mother at times insisted that she should sit next to the bath, so she could save her in case of a heart attack, although this was entirely imaginary.

Apart from the fact that we have found these mothers' exhibitionism to have been directed towards this one child in particular, we can see that an additional disturbing factor lies in their display of real or fantasied damage: the scars, blood, fear of fatness, fear of heart attacks. Through this the children's own fantasies of being damaged had been severely reinforced. We also find that by being made to look and experience the mother's castration fantasies, the children's sadistic fantasies and consequent guilt feelings had become closely linked with the functions of looking and learning.

In the initial interview, the boys' mothers had described the close, loving bond that existed between them and their children. My more intimate knowledge of them showed that indeed these mothers were able to sense their children's needs and to understand them to an astonishing degree. Closer knowledge showed, however, that the mothers' capacity to understand their children was confined to certain areas only—areas in which the child played the role unconsciously assigned to him and was therefore a means towards his mother's satisfaction. When faced with reactions in the child that were threatening the mother's fantasies and hindering her wish fulfillment, her understanding of the child's feelings and needs became completely blocked. The child's anxiety was then utterly disregarded.

To give examples: the boys' failure to become independent and to stand up for themselves did not trouble the mothers; their sadness, weakness and fears were met with deep sympathy. They comforted the boys by means of oral satisfactions mainly: by food, sweets and kisses; they took them on their laps, cuddled them and took them into bed, as if they were still small babies. The boys' tendency to regress and to fall ill was met with as much nursing and comfort as could have been wished for by the child; but the slightest signs of independence, of curiosity about the mother's affairs, of criticism or aggression against the mother could neither be understood nor tolerated. Any sign that the child was forming a close attachment to someone else, even the father, was at once interfered with. The child's negative feelings against the mother had been completely suppressed from an early period on; any critical functions concerning her person were equally absent. When I first knew my patients, these feelings were not countered by aggression but were dealt with by providing more satisfying experiences. By non-verbal means, but also in words, the children had been given to understand that safety was to be found only in close unity with the mother. This I have found to include a double threat: the children had come to feel that any move away from or against the mother would expose not only them, but also the mother, to danger. Their guilt and anxiety concerning the mother's state of mind, health and life weighed heavily on these children. This was not only the result of their unconscious hostility and fantasies about what might happen to mother, but it had become so strong because the child really *saw* his mother's sadness, tears and bodily symptoms as soon as he did not conform to the role assigned to him.

To keep the child passive and stupid was a necessity for these mothers, whose anxiety increased intolerably as soon as they felt that they were 'losing' the child. This is the situation described by Mahler (1942), who drew attention to the following important function of pseudo stupidity: not to know or feel what the mother cannot tolerate the child to know or feel is necessary because both mother and child need the stupidity in order to retain the pre-verbal, bodily satisfaction of their early relationship. It is evident that where such a situation exists, a normal oedipal development cannot be expected.

A mother who exercises such overwhelming power over a child is felt to be not only a loving and safe mother, but also a dangerous, castrating mother. For the boys, therefore, the move to the phallic and genital levels was doomed to failure. Nicky and Jimmy expressed these fantasies in terms of a dangerous, biting vagina. In these fantasies Jimmy's repressed knowledge of his mother's promiscuity became clearly visible for the first time.

For the full understanding of mothers and children, it is important to try and form a picture of the children's fathers, as far as they had played a part in the children's lives.

Even with the little we know about these women, we are justified to doubt their capacity to form and maintain a normal relationship with a man. As has been pointed out, the leading fantasy they had in common, and verbalized repeatedly, was concerned with the disappointments and rejections they had experienced in the oedipal phase. The true story of their lives, as I came to know it eventually, could be entitled: 'In Search of a Loving Father.' We know that the repeated failure to find the fulfillment of this fantasy is based on the failure of a normal oedipal relation and the consequent failure to adjust to femininity.

I now want to give some details about Jimmy's and Nicky's fathers: We know that Jimmy's father had condoned the presence of a lover. According to his wife, he had enjoyed his presence. This may have been true to some extent. There is no doubt, however, that he suffered deeply from his wife's need for other men, but he was too passive to take action and quietly submitted to the role assigned to him, taking on all the tasks of cooking and child care that accumulated upon him whenever she left for weekends and holidays. He repeatedly said that he would put up with anything rather than separate from his wife. She, too, could not imagine life without him, and the similarity between her relationship with her husband and the one with the child was striking.

Seen as an object for identification, we find little that could have helped Jimmy in his masculine development. He identified with the father's weakness, passivity and unreserved love for the mother. He did not see the father as a rival, nor as an ally against other rivals. When he had become able to think critically, he showed how puzzled he was about his father's role. He once said to me: 'You think, perhaps, that he is the biggest man you know, but I tell you he is really made of cardboard.' Jimmy loved his father, and in this love the features of the pre-oedipal mother relationship were prominent. He wanted to be mothered by the father and, indeed, he found in him an admirable substitute for her, who comforted him whenever they were left to share their sadness about her unfaithfulness.

In the boys' thumb sucking, fellatio fantasies played a prominent role.

Nicky's chance of finding support in identification with his father was no greater. He first met his father—or, rather, the man presumed to be his father—when he was seven years

old. He therefore played no part in Nicky's early development as a love object, nor with regard to his identification.
He played a very large part, however, as a fantasy object. The
fantasies Nicky had built up around him were closely related
to the mother's fantasies about him, as far as they were
known to me. For her he was a fantastically frightening and
revengeful figure, and most of her pseudological productions
were centred around him and his imagined hate of her. Even
without her analyst's confirmation, it would have been easy
to recognize the similarity of her dramatic accounts about
her father and her first husband.

Nicky entirely shared the fantasies about the father as a
dangerous persecutor, whereas he professed to love the stepfather unreservedly. Questions about him were answered
monotonously by him with the sentence: 'He is more of a
father than my real father.' This was the mother's sentence,
which he had taken over. He *had* to know and feel about him,
too, what the mother wanted him to know and feel. In fact,
the father withdrew from them but was again and again
provoked into situations that forced him into the role of an
enemy. These two cases show in some detail what I also found
in the others: in the course of the children's development, the
father was either absent or, where he was present, not *he* but
another man was the mother's love object. We are well
acquainted with the pathogenic effect of the father's absence
or of changing father figures in the oedipal phase from our
observations in the Hampstead Nurseries. This has been
discussed and vividly illustrated by Anna Freud and
Dorothy Burlingham in *Infants without Families* (1944).

On the basis of the foregoing it will be clear that these
analyses presented considerable technical problems. In
every child's analysis the conflict of loyalties between parents and analyst plays an important part. In her paper 'Child
analysis and the mother', Dorothy Burlingham (1935b)
described how manifold and serious these obstacles can be.

With the close knowledge of their children that these
mothers possessed, they had, of course, sensed every change

in their children: their growing attachment to the analyst, the beginning of the uncovering of repressed negative feelings, and the capacity to see and experience reality independently. While they naturally appreciated the improvement in as far as learning at school was concerned, they found it increasingly difficult to bear their child's recovery where the relationship with him was affected. They counteracted progress in many ways, by seducing the child back into the early relationship, openly criticizing the analyst or producing obstacles in more subtle ways. Decisive progress was made each time the mothers were away.

In the last stage of the treatment, a critical phase occurred in each case, caused by uncovering of the special aspects of the three mothers' disturbances, which I consider to have played an important part in the children's disturbances: *the mother's compulsive lying and deliberate withholding of secrets.*

It will be remembered that Jimmy, Nicky and Bettina had been causing considerable anxiety by lying. This symptom had upset their mothers far more than any other sign of their disturbance. The children's compulsion to lie had soon shown itself in the transference, when at first it was not easy to distinguish from the mechanism of denial. Gradually, elaborate fantasy stories made their appearance. Nicky's and Jimmy's lies were of a similar nature. Two main types of stories, the aims of which were denial of castration anxiety and fantasied wish fulfillment regarding a peaceful home life with an ideal mother, were told or acted in daily life and in their treatment. From the transference it could gradually be seen that the children knew about their mother's untruthfulness. At the same time, recent observations revived early memories, which made it clear that they suspected the mother of keeping a secret from them.

In the mothers' pseudological productions, too, it was possible to trace two leading themes: they contained accounts of men's great, unfailing love and kindness, or of excessively cruel treatment they had to endure. The change in these fantasies seemed closely related to phases of elation and depression. Bettina's stories had the same content: from every bus ride or shopping expedition she brought accounts of having been showered with presents, having had prices of goods reduced by kind, smiling men, or having been shouted at or attacked by dangerous men. These stories were at times almost identical with her mother's stories, though less subtle in their construction.

We find here the situation that had been so clearly formulated by Helene Deutsch (1922): 'Pseudologia is a daydream told another person as reality. The lie serves the purpose of reversing reality where disappointment has been experienced and in it we find the trace of an early, real experience; reactivated, experienced, as well as told, *as if* they were true.'

The first doubts about the mother's trustworthiness were regressively expressed in oral terms by Nicky and Jimmy. Nicky went through a phase when he spent all his pocket money on meringues, buying two in each shop on the way from the station to me. We had to eat them simultaneously and find out whether they were 'real' or 'swindle'. If he thought that the shoplady had been honest, he was overjoyed. Those that he thought were 'swindled', he violently destroyed and spat out, and he abused the shoplady in strong terms. This followed a phase in which he had aggressively demanded food from me but rejected it even before it was given, saying that what I could offer would never be reliably good, doubting that it contained the right ingredients, asking for details of recipes. Through this he became able to express observations about discrepancies between reality and his mother's statements. Disbelief in *any* statement she made followed this phase.

Nicky brought similar material, with the added feature that he could neither believe in her nor ever know where she was at any given time.

Bettina expressed her doubts through examining jewellery for its true value, accusing her mother of cheating, pretending that things were made of gold and that she possessed jewellery which in fact she had only borrowed. She developed a compulsion to add the words: 'honestly', or 'it's real, I swear', to any statement she made.

After the first outbursts of anger against the mother, Nicky and Jimmy became depressed and cried a great deal, reacting with mourning to the loss of the ideal mother of their babyhood. They were no longer able to respond in the former way to the infantile comfort she offered them. As a love object for their beginning heterosexual feelings she was too dangerous, especially for Nicky who was now so near adolescence. They withdrew from her and turned to their fathers.

In all cases a great part of the inhibitions that had caused severe school problems had been much improved long before the material about the mother's untruthfulness was accessible. The analysis of oral and anal aggression, of looking and the masturbation fantasies connected with this material had opened up the way to sublimations.

For normal functioning, however, it became urgent for them to get real proof of the correctness of their suspicions that their mother was deliberately deceiving them. Jimmy was now convinced that his mother had had many successive relationships with men, and he especially remembered one she had when he was a small child. It was clear that he had made many observations during the oedipal phase, having been considered too small to notice what was going on, and that his apparent stupidity had given him the chance to see many things.

Nicky suspected his mother of having deceived the father, while he had always been told that it was the father who had left her. He remembered scenes and statements made by people and became convinced that the man said to be his father was not in fact his father.

Bettina, in turn, became able to remember her father and also another man who had been important in her mother's life before they left the country.

As the children progressed in freeing themselves from their repressions and began to recover early memories, as they detached themselves from identification with the mother's symptoms and began to feel true affects in accordance with their experiences, the mothers reacted with anger, depression and illness. Their open hostility turned against the analyst, and they threatened to break off treatment when the children demanded to know the truth. Nicky's and Jimmy's fathers insisted that treatment be continued: Bettina's treatment was officially terminated, but she continued it for six months without the mother's knowledge.

With the father's help, the mother finally decided to tell Jimmy that his memories were correct and that there had been many men she had loved simultaneously with his father.

Through his father, Nicky learned the truth about his mother's unfaithfulness to him. These facts had led both boys to doubts about the identity of their father. Finally Nicky asked his father whether he or another man was his father. He was told that in fact neither of them knew for certain.

Bettina, who now remembered many details about her father, insisted that her mother should tell her whether she was sure that her husband had died in a concentration camp before she decided to remarry and made it quite clear to her that she remembered a man friend of the mother's, with whom she had deceived the father while Bettina was between three and four years old.

We can now see that the confession made in the initial interview had served the purpose of hiding facts of an earlier phase in their lives, about which the guilt was far greater. In the fact of the promiscuity that had led to the uncertain paternity in the boys' cases, one can probably find the answer to the problem why these children were so much closer to the mothers than their other children. The closeness of the link was based, to a large extent, on the guilt that the children personified for them.

An important problem emerges from these facts—namely, the question of the effect on the developing ego functions of reality testing and synthesis and of the building up of memory in cases where the mechanisms used by the mother directly interfere with the normal establishment of these functions in the child. When children in the oedipal phase are exposed to the nature and intensity of experiences as were found in these cases, the need for avoidance of instinctual danger, both of the aggressive and of the sexual kind, is a necessity, and far-reaching repression, interfering with memory, must be expected.

In the normal process of reality testing, the external world, represented in the first place by the mother, has an important function. As Anna Freud (1936) has pointed out, it is common in our dealings with younger children to use denial or fall in with their own use of this mechanism in order to help them overcome painful experiences; but this is strictly confined to limited conditions, and the child is again confronted with reality afterwards.

When the mother's capacity to test reality is impaired in certain areas, when she herself uses the mechanism of denial in word and act, the child's attempts to distinguish reality from fantasy meet with a serious obstacle. Instead of helping him on the way out of confusion, she creates new confusion, and we find that fantasy life continues to play an excessive part and helps to create the appearance of stupidity.

In the boys' cases, it appears that the intimate, satisfying pre-oedipal relationship became severely threatened as soon as the intellectual functions, permitting reality testing in relation to the mother, had sufficiently matured. The observations seem to show that the first perceptions of the divergence between reality and what Nicky used to call 'mother's reality' had been experienced as a shock. Identification with the mother's untruthfulness—namely, with the very aspect that would have caused her to be given up as a love object—was the consequence, and the satisfying mother of the oral phase could be retained.

Similarly, the child's discovery of the mother's secret causes a severe rejection when it is first encountered. In an interesting paper on the psychology of secrecy, Alfred Gross (1936) considers the effect upon the child of meeting a secret in the mother in the following way: 'When encountering the secret in the parent, the child experiences a double rejection on the emotional and on the mental levels. It relinquishes the person as a love object and identifies with the very feature which has caused the rejection, regressing simultaneously to the level on which danger arising from the secret is no longer a threat.'

To sum up: In the cases observed, material was brought to show the part played by the mothers in relation to the children's disturbances. In the absence of analytic material, observations were confined to interviews with the mothers with corroboration from the fathers and from the children's analyses. The mothers' part in the establishment of oral fixations and their influence on the fate of the component instincts of curiosity and looking were discussed, and it was shown which circumstances had made it impossible for the children to enter latency and develop sublimations successfully. The symptomatology of mothers and children was found to be similar, owing to the children's identification with their mother's symptoms.

From the few facts about the mothers' histories, from the content of their pseudological productions, from their relationships to men, and from their way of dealing with their children, one is justified in concluding that they have themselves failed to adjust normally to their femininity and that a great part of their disturbance has the function of deceiving themselves and others about this fact.

The cases show close similarity to the well-known structure of pseudo imbecility and learning inhibitions. An additional factor in establishing the symptom was found in the mothers' symptom of lying and secretiveness, which reinforced the impairment of the children's ego functions of memory, reality testing and synthesizing.

CHAPTER THIRTEEN

Neurotic learning disturbance and subsequent maladjustment at work

with Liselotte Frankl

I n the step from school to work, at the point of choice of a career, aptitude and motivation have to be considered. But even if both of these have been found adequate, success and satisfaction at work are often absent, since internal conflicts from the past that are revived in the present can interfere with the chosen career.

The application of knowledge derived from psychoanalysis seems to have an important place at the point when young people have to take the step from school to work and the decision about the choice of career has to be made.

Almost every case in treatment gives us the opportunity to study the motivations for entry into a training or career. The interaction between an individual's potential capacities for successful adjustment to his chosen work and the elements in his personality that tend to hinder this become clarified. Psychoanalytic treatment aims at preventing that in the chosen career neurotic conflicts that arouse anxiety and guilt interfere excessively with reality adaptation and satisfaction.

Our material comes from a variety of cases: some of these had been in treatment while still at school, and the various internal and external factors leading to the actual choice of work had been followed for some time. Others began treatment after recently entering a career. The third main source is derived from adults in whose analysis the elements leading up to their choice of career and the subsequent fate of their lives in this career could be traced. The part played by the nature of an adolescent's relationship to his parents, his identifications, competition, submission, revolt, etc., are of great importance in understanding the multiple aspects of the problems that have to be solved at this point. Knowledge based on clinical experience of this kind can be useful to those who have to deal with young people at the stage when decisions have to be made which will influence their future. In the selection of applicants for jobs or training, or in counselling, an approach based on this knowledge proves helpful and gives the opportunity further to check on its usefulness.

As an example of the manner in which neurotic conflicts can interfere with functioning at work and in training, we have chosen the case of a girl aged 17 of good intelligence (IQ 125), whose long-standing wish to become a teacher was interfered with by a number of obstacles that led to her failing her final school exams. In the course of her treatment, the factors responsible for her learning disturbance became clarified; their effect on her school achievements and on the training she eventually obtained could be traced and the interferences alleviated.

Jessy came into psychoanalytic treatment at the beginning of a career that had been decided on by her mother and stepfather. The material reported emerged in the course of her analysis, which lasted four years. Her own wish had been to enter a Training College for Teachers in order to become a Nursery and Infant teacher. However, after her school failure, her parents decided that she should start work as soon as possible. As the mother was successful as a dressmaker and cutter and Jessy seemed good at dressmaking, her parents decided that she should be apprenticed to a firm of which they knew the Manager. Jessy was angry and disappointed that her wish to become a teacher was disregarded.

At the end of one year of dressmaking, Jessy had reached a point when she felt unable to carry on.

Phase 1:
failure at work

At the time of referral, Jessy felt that, in contrast to her previous personality, she had changed into a listless, angry person. Her relationship to her stepfather was alternating between withdrawal from him and violent outbursts of aggression in which she accused him of ruining her life by forcing her to do work that she did not want to do. She made more and more mistakes at work rather than improve through experience. She hated her boss.

Of the various aspects of the failure of her career, as seen in her treatment, the following played an outstanding part:

(1)   Jessy's extreme anger about having to submit to her stepfather's wish was by no means the beginning but, rather, the final manifestation of aggressive feelings and phantasies that had been directed against him. She had grown up without a father, had never known him nor been given information about him, and had built up a phantasy picture of an ideal, kind and loving father. This was shattered by the reality of the stepfather. Although not unkind, he was rigid in his views and expected his decisions to be accepted. He consequently became an exaggeratedly bad father in Jessy's phantasy, and all her anger about the unknown father's failure to care for her was displaced onto the stepfather.

In her work this anger was soon shifted onto the man who was in charge of the workshop. She resented his presence, felt unjustly treated, responded to him either by passive resistance or open aggressive behaviour and finally by unconsciously making more and more serious mistakes in cutting material, wasting yards and yards of cloth, through which he suffered considerable damage.

It was possible to trace the nature of the cutting errors to phantasies connected with her conflicts about men in general, and the activity of cutting as a phantasied aggressive attack against them.

(2)   A further reason for Jessy's failure to adjust to the work of dressmaking was found in another aspect of her phantasies about her unknown father: she feared that he had been a vulgar, low-class man, and much of her behaviour and her thinking was motivated by the need to prove to herself and others that this had not been the case. To become a teacher was, among other reasons, so important to her as it meant that she would enter into a professional career, a clear definite step away from the danger of being a working-class girl. She was unable to mix with the other girls at work and felt so strongly about this that she kept herself separate and refused to go up in the lift or to have meals with them.

(3)   Her wish to outdo her mother who was a successful dressmaker and cutter and her simultaneous fear of succeeding in this wish formed a major obstacle. She imagined that her mother would not be able to tolerate it if she became as good or better at the same work. Her guilt contributed to her failure. Since her mother's marriage when Jessy was adolescent, she had no longer felt loved and wanted by her, and her wish to take revenge because she was born illegitimate and had been brought up in a residential nursery became overwhelmingly strong at times. Her self-esteem had been low since she had understood the meaning of illegitimacy and the idea that no one could think of her as a worthwhile person had begun when she had come to live with the mother and met children who had normal homes. Her failure at school and at work had added to the conviction that she was worthless. These experiences of despair resulted partly in aggressive behaviour towards the hated people, partly in withdrawal from them.

Initially she had made external circumstances entirely responsible for her failure, and the first phase of her treatment had largely to deal with the task of making her aware of the defensive nature of her accusations and gradually to recognize the part played by her own conflicts.

Phase 2:
change from the hated work
to the chosen career

Jessy's parents were very disturbed by her reaction to her first job. Her depressive moods as well as her aggressive behaviour towards them led to their decision to allow her to take the Montessori School Training she wished for, and which did not require school leaving examinations.

This decision brought immediate relief, and it seemed to the parents and to a large extent also to Jessy that all problems were solved once the external pressure was removed. During the interval between the end of her work as a dressmaker and the beginning of the nursery school training, she felt that her parents were 'good' as they had finally fulfilled her wish. There was now no longer any authoritative figure to be afraid of or to fight against. The anxieties concerning her social class could be avoided, once she stopped having to mix with working class girls; the step into teaching meant that she was now establishing herself in the professional class.

It seems important to describe this favourable change in some detail, as such situational changes are often regarded as 'cures' or as the therapeutic interventions most indicated for adolescents who experience similar problems at this stage. While it is true that in this, as in other cases, the reactive elements of the symptomatology diminish when external pressure is removed, it is most deceptive, as this case shows, to regard such improvements as indications that the adolescent's problems have been satisfactorily dealt with. Such conclusions can only be drawn if follow-up work is not carried out over any relevant length of time. The degree to which situational changes have a more than temporary effect depends, of course, on the adolescent's psychopathology and on the degree of internalization of the conflicts that have led to his disturbance.

Phase 3:
teacher's training and first teaching job

Soon after the Montessori training course began, it became the stage for Jessy's renewed anxieties. Gradually her conflicts and attempts to deal with them reappeared. Phantasies about teachers and colleagues and fluctuations in her self-esteem soon transformed the idealized course. Jessy came to understand that her problems were not mainly imposed by hated people and circumstances in the external world but were to a large extent her inner problems, which she externalized and therefore re-experienced in the new settings.

A large factor in the difficulties she experienced during the year of study was caused by the learning inhibition that now reappeared in all its aspects and clarified her failure to get the school-leaving exam.

Among the features leading to the school failure were an intensity of repression shown in an unusually extensive infantile amnesia, which interfered with her capacity to remember facts she had to learn. The infantile amnesia was found to be combined of a variety of factors, of which only a few are mentioned here.

As in other cases of children brought up in residential nurseries, Jessy showed a scarcity of distinct memories concerning people, places and events. Even though she had fortunately been able to see her mother daily, it appears that the large number of changing adults and children contributed to the indistinct picture she had retained of her past. Confusion interfered with her capacity to think and remember clearly and therefore affected her learning.

Her mother's psychopathology, which made it impossible for her to talk to her children about her own and their past, had led to confusion and uncertainty about the patient's father, and this resulted in confusion about her own identity. These factors are all known to interfere with the capacity to learn, to retain a clear, well-organized picture of what has been taken in and to be capable of reproducing knowledge. Interferences caused by disturbed relationships, of course, play an additional important role. Jessy's phantasies about examinations showed the intense conflicts relating to her wish to 'beat' everyone, and her guilt had a paralysing effect on her performance. Analytic work brought her sufficient insight to deal with the major problems of work and exams in a favourable way, and she obtained the Montessori Diploma. However, her first teaching job and her actual work with children brought new aspects of her problems to the fore.

Jessy began to realize that her problems through which her work was most hindered lay mainly in two areas. The first was well known to us from her training, where the women in authority had been the centre of all her aggressive feelings, and this had inhibited her thinking and her activities. In her first job, the headmistress and the older colleagues now took over this role in her mind, and she was unable to deal with her class whenever she imagined that one of them would come and see her at her work.

Her aggressive impulses hindered her work also in another area, which had previously not been noticeable. She found it extremely difficult to keep discipline in her classroom, and at times the situation with the group of children she was in charge of became quite chaotic. She felt paralysed and close to tears at such moments, and by this behaviour the feared situation was brought about: the headmistress had to come to restore order, thus implying criticism of her. The analysis showed that what inhibited her to the extent of 'paralysis' was the immense aggressive impulse that came over her 'like a wave'. She wanted to shout, rush up to the unruly children, shake them and hit everybody. Memories of her childhood in the residential nursery where she had been one of the rushing crowd came at this time, and the revival of her early aggressive outbursts played a large part in this phase. Gradually further work showed interferences with her capacity to function as a teacher through the intense feelings of likes and dislikes that different types of children aroused in her. Gradually the treatment enabled her to bring these likes and dislikes of children under more conscious control. Thereby she became a teacher who could give all types of children a more adequate emotional climate, neither making them experience her dislike nor over-stimulating them by excessive attention.

In the case of physical illness, one aims at early spotting and provides constant care in order to reduce ill effects and the possible interferences with normal functioning to a minimum. In the same way, attempts should be made to treat neurotic interferences with work and life tasks in the early stages, otherwise men and women struggle through life, doing work that is unsuited and unsatisfying to them; they may finally drift into the group of people classed as unemployable, as a result of psychosomatic illness or chronic neurosis, or even end as cases of unexplained suicide. Teachers and school psychologists who are in constant touch with school children's learning and working problems are in a position to differentiate between the many who can work their way out of such a phase and those so hindered that the remark 'could do better if she really tried' is unlikely to be helpful because the obstacles are beyond conscious control. In cases where interferences with learning and with social relationships have not been overcome earlier, they are likely to form a serious obstacle in the early phase of the adolescent's working life. If more facilities for diagnosis and treatment were available at this stage, a great deal of preventive work could still be done. It is our impression that in carefully selected adolescent cases, especially in late adolescence, much can still be done to prevent chronic, permanent dissatisfaction and inefficiency at work.

CHAPTER FOURTEEN

Dorothy Burlingham
and her work

I n the same year as the paper 'Child analysis and the mother' (Burlingham, 1935b) was published, the paper 'Empathy between infant and mother' appeared in *Imago*.

In its introduction, Dorothy Burlingham refers to the earlier publication and says that empathy between infant and mother has continued to engage her interest and that the new paper is devoted to the same problem. She makes a clear differentiation between the developmental studies of academic psychology as they were then carried out at Yale and in Vienna, which referred primarily to the infant's observational abilities, and her own interest, which refers to the affects and their development in relation to the growing capacity to receive stimuli and to assimilate observations.

Bulletin of the Hampstead Clinic (1980), 3:80–84.

She offers a large number of subtle observations that show that babies and young children are able to sense their mother's state of mind much earlier than was commonly thought. Responses to facial expression, to voice and posture often show that they have recognized feelings in their mother of which she herself may have been unaware at the time, or which she was attempting to keep hidden.

Here Mrs Burlingham also discusses observations of the ways in which various instinctual needs of the mother reach the child and may stimulate it and how certain areas of the child's body are affected, as he experiences oral, anal or genital excitation, gratification or frustration in response to the mother's own satisfactions, her anxieties or inhibitions.

Her continued interest in the interplay between child and mother, which she formulated in the 1930s, is essential for the understanding of her research throughout her life.

No one could have formulated this more simply and clearly than she did herself. In the preface to the volume *Psychoanalytic Studies of the Sighted and the Blind,* published in 1972, which contains 17 of her papers, she says:

> ... the articles collected in this book may seem to be in the nature of a haphazard assembly of presentations giving evidence of an analyst and child analyst changing subjects of interest during a lifetime of work. In fact, this impression is misleading. Even though the concern is with apparently differing subjects, my main interest was always concentrated on a major point: the relationship between mother and child.

In the paper 'Empathy between infant and mother', she not only deals with observations of pre-verbal and non-verbal communications, she also raises the questions concerning the ways in which such communications may occur. Among them the problem of telepathy is referred to. Mrs Burlingham says:

> Whenever an affect or an idea appears simultaneously in two partners, one gains the impression that the process in question is a telepathic one, but this has yet to be proved.

She refers to instances known to many people when it was clear that mother and child were occupied with the same problem at the same time, and she tells of her own experiences when she was in analysis simultaneously with her children and was struck by the fact that a subject that had played a major part in her own analysis was at the same time important in an analysis of one of her children. It became clear that the problem was considered of interest in discussions among analysts at the time. It was taken up by Freud in the *New Introductory Lectures* (1933), where he refers to Mrs Burlingham's remarks on this topic. He says in the chapter on 'Dreams and occultism',

> If there is such a thing as telepathy as a real process, we may suspect that, in spite of its being so hard to demonstrate, it is quite a common phenomenon. It would tally with our expectations if we were able to point to it particularly in the mental life of children.

And he goes on to say:

> A short time ago Dorothy Burlingham, a trustworthy witness [in the original text: *eine vertrauenswürdige Frau*], in a paper on child analysis and the mother [1932] published some observations which, if they can be confirmed, would be bound to put an end to the remaining doubts on the reality of thought-transference.

In her concluding remarks on the paper on empathy, Mrs Burlingham refers to the problem once more. Summarizing the observations on empathy, she feels that compared with the helplessness and ignorance one experiences with telepathic explanations, one feels on safe and familiar ground once it can be demonstrated that an unexpectedly early phase of acute and lively observation, perceptiveness and receptivity can be the basis of communication between infant and mother.

In the preface from which I quoted earlier, Mrs Burlingham also refers to her study of twins. She says:

I moved [from the study of empathy between mother and infant] to the opposite, i.e. to a rather unusual disturbance of the close mother–infant tie through the constant presence of a third in that partnership which is usually confined to two people: to twins. Since it has been my good fortune to explore several pairs of twins, either in analytic treatment or supervision, or observation, I was able to show that subtle but fateful repercussion in the individual's love life, in cases where the first object relationship is made, not to the mother, but to a peer.

The paper, 'A study of identical twins, their analytic material compared with existing observation data of their early childhood', written jointly with Arthur Barron, gives evidence of this point, which was pursued further in the book on *Twins* (1952).

The first chapter of this book: 'A study of three pairs of identical twins', deals with the fantasy of having a twin. Mrs Burlingham here draws attention to a daydream frequently found in latency children, a conscious fantasy resulting from disappointment of the oedipal situation. The imaginary twin's function is 'to supply a partner who will provide an escape from solitude and loneliness'. Dorothy Burlingham shows how the Family Romance discussed by Freud and animal fantasies referred to by Anna Freud and Kate Friedlander originate in the same way. She then discusses some well-known stories in literature, where this theme is elaborated, as in Little Lord Fauntleroy and his dog who helps him overcome his longing for his mother, and the twins in Thornton Wilder's *Bridge of San Luis Rey*. The absolute identity of appearance, a secret language and telepathy between them are common occurrences. Difficulties relating to homosexual fears and the disturbance of the twin relationship when one of them falls in love with a girl are all to be found in literature. Dorothy Burlingham here points to a further important element in twin fantasies: the role of narcissism. A child cannot imagine finding anyone more satisfactory than he is himself. He therefore creates a twin, an image of himself that he can love. Here self-love appears under the mask of object-love.

A further use of twin fantasies lies in the expression of discord and unity within the personality itself, as found in examples of twins representing ambivalent tendencies and opposite instinctual wishes of various kinds.

The main trends underlying the formation of twin fantasies in the thwarted lonely latency child and the comparison of elements in these fantasies with the evidence found through direct observation or in later analytic material are of the greatest interest.

Following the introductory chapter on twin fantasies, we find the fascinating observational material and its elaboration, which gives us insight into the developmental progress of each of the twins: Jessy and Bessy, admitted to the War Nurseries at the age of 4½ months in July 1941, the boy twins admitted 7 months later, also aged 4 months, and, in the following year, the 3½-year-old girls. Mrs Burlingham took a very active part in planning the setting for them at the Nursery throughout the four years of their lives with us, in the way they were handled and the manner in which observations were collected and recorded. She spent much time watching them herself and read and discussed all observation cards written by staff and students. While they were babies, Sister Sofie Dann, who had devised the developmental charts and the charts on sleep, regularly discussed these with Mrs Burlingham.

Anyone who has taken the time not only to read the book but to look at the charts in some detail will have become aware of the amount of thought given to every small point that lent itself to observation and comparison and of the intensity of work that went into the study.

It could not be foreseen at the time that many years' follow-up material on the twins was to be available and that one of the twin boys is actually still in contact with the nurse his twin brother had been attached to as a toddler. The follow-up has made the most unusual and instructive study

possible, which Dorothy Burlingham published with Arthur
Barron, who had the boys in his Home for problem children
and who had both boys in analysis with him.

Follow-up work right up to the present time has been
possible also with the girl-twins Bessy and Jessy, now aged
39. One of these twins had an analysis with me in adolescence, and the other was analysed by Miss Schnurmann. As a
result of problems arising in Bessy's marriage, she returned
for a few months' treatment with me three years ago, and
these problems, which I discussed with Mrs Burlingham at
the time, threw a great deal of light on the twin relationship.

Much valuable insight was gained from these studies on
the very question Mrs Burlingham had posed initially concerning the interference through the twinship with the relationship to the mother. Much new insight was gained, too,
into the pathology of personality development through the
constant presence of a being so like oneself, leading to hatred
and guilt, the wish to destroy and—as seen in the girls—a
constant longing to be reunited. Also their relationship to
their husbands showed features clearly influenced by the
twinship, creating unusual problems.

Here the similarities and differences between twin fantasies and the reality of having a twin became clear.

Dorothy Burlingham's sensitive understanding of the
many aspects of observation within these studies was
remarkable. She was helped in this by her special gift for
empathy, which we experienced in her on so many occasions
and which was probably heightened by the fact that she
herself had older twin sisters.

Although a great deal is left to be said on the twin studies,
I now want to turn to the studies of the simultaneous treatment of mother and child. The setting up of the project began
in 1950. It was the natural continuation of her wish to enter
more deeply into the paths of communication between child
and mother. Her interest in material derived from simultaneous analysis was already apparent nearly 20 years

earlier, in 1934, when she quoted a verbal communication made by Berta Bornstein who had a mother–child couple in treatment with her.

The *method* of simultaneous analysis was devised by Mrs Burlingham. For each mother-and-child couple, a team of three analysts is needed: one each for the treatment of the mother and the child, and a third who is referred to as 'the co-ordinator'. The need to find a way of bringing the material of both analyses together without influencing the work of each analyst was felt to be of great importance.

For the first case that was systematically co-ordinated (and subsequently published in 1955), Dorothy Burlingham introduced a system whereby both the mother's and the child's analysts reported to her on the work done each week, in addition to which a weekly written report was made available to her. This method, based on the experience of case supervision, was then adopted for all other cases, with the exception of one in which the mother's analyst also acted as co-ordinator.

The case of Bobby and his mother, who were analysed by Alice Goldberger and André Lussier, was published in *The Psychoanalytic Study of the Child* (Burlingham, Goldberger & Lussier, 1955).

The co-ordinator's role involves an unwavering concentration on listening, finding links, tracing back to particular interaction and following the fate of common trends in the material of both mother and child.

One of the most important findings in simultaneous analysis relates to *the mother's fantasies as a pathogenic factor*.

In the case of Bobby and his mother, Mrs Burlingham has distinguished between the effect on the child of those of the mother's fantasies that were communicated to him mainly in words, and others where he was involved in the violent acting-out of her fantasies and was physically stimulated by her. She found that, in the former case, where he was influenced by his mother's fantasies and their communication had remained essentially verbal, analysis was able to free him from their effect. Although they had originated in the mother's unconscious, such fantasies had become his own, had undergone elaborations of his own and could be dealt with analytically in the usual way. Analytical work led to differentiation of his own and his mother's need to maintain these fantasies and to the gradual growth of his independence from her.

In the latter case, however, where Bobby was involved in fantasies that were acted out by the mother, the outcome was found to be less favourable. This was true especially with regard to continued physical stimulation of the child's body. This mother had been compelled to handle Bobby's genitals, and these seductions continually renewed his close physical tie to her and tended to counteract the analytical work.

In her conclusion, Dorothy Burlingham suggested that it might be helpful to bear these distinctions in mind whenever we have to assess the chances of freeing a child by analysis from the pathogenic influence of his mother's disturbance.

Since work on this case was concluded, we have had the opportunity to make further observations on this problem. They have confirmed her conclusions. I have been a co-ordinator in the treatment of four mother–child couples. These cases have shown in detail how the mother's fantasies that are acted out physically with the child constitute a major pathogenic factor. Fixation points are firmly established and maintained by the mother's continued seductions. Premature and continued excitation experienced passively have caused severe interference with normal development.

The amount of analytic work needed to understand and work through the ramifications of the mother's fantasies that compel her to use her child for her own gratification make it clear why cases of this kind are not responding to more superficial forms of psychotherapy. They lead to aspects of the mother's childhood material that come to light only under considerable difficulty, even in intensive treatment. In such cases prolonged work is needed until the mother is able to free herself from these unconscious conflicts, which force her to equate the child in fantasy with an aspect of herself or an object of her past.

Ten simultaneous analyses have been carried out so far. From the brief description I have given, I hope it has become clear how important for so many of us who were her co-workers and for our students has been the part played by Mrs Burlingham over the years. In the general area of empathy and the application of this approach to the specific topics I have dealt with, a lasting change in our understanding has been reached through the studies inspired by Dorothy Burlingham.

Postscript

An analyst at eighty

I t is striking but undeniable that many psychoanalysts go on working long after members of other professions have taken retirement. It is far from clear to me why this should be so, though I have thought about it on many occasions. Certainly my age has not altered the fact that there are many people with personal problems who want to talk to me about them, and it continues to surprise and please me that these include people of all ages. I find it important to keep in touch with past and present students, with many younger people entering our discipline and with changing and developing ideas. It helps me to feel that I still have a useful part to play, it fosters a feeling of independence and it provides a sense of personal value that counteracts the loss of self-esteem from which so many ageing people suffer.

During the past ten years I have been particularly interested in patients' responses to my growing older, often expressed in concern about my health, and many patients look for changes feared or wished for. Some colleagues take the view that the reality of the analyst's appearance, age, gender or discernible circumstances has no bearing on the nature of the transference within the framework of the analysis itself. The last few years have convinced me that this is by no means the case. Many years ago, when I was pregnant, I had reason to be convinced that my condition had a bearing on my patients' transference responses, though one seminar leader told me at the time that the fact that my pregnancy was visible would not affect the transference material.

The last ten years have only strengthened my conviction. It would be a mistake, however, to think that all transference concerns about my age are linked with fears of loss. Just as often, they involve hostile wishes and fantasies, together with the intense guilt associated with them. A patient who had been extremely hostile towards me in one session brought to the next a dream in which I had died. When he left the session, he thought he noticed how much older and weaker I looked. He was troubled all weekend by thoughts that I might die, and when he returned to his analysis on the Monday, it was with the greatest relief that he saw that I was still there. Although wishes and fantasies of an identical kind occur in patients of any age, they are often much more accessible and easily available with an older analyst and do not necessarily need the same intensive defence analysis before they become accessible. On the other hand, conscious sexual feelings about the analyst are much less directly experienced or easily expressed. One patient, for example, always thought of me as a 'granny' and observed, with some truth, that it was difficult for him to think of himself in bed with his granny except when he was a little boy and she looked after him when his mother was away.

Almost all analysts who have worked with adolescents have taken the view that there are problems if an adolescent girl is treated by a good-looking young man, or if an adolescent boy is treated by a pretty young woman. And yet I had often thought that it must be difficult for a young person to talk with confidence to someone who was very much older. In practice, I have not found this to be the case. On one occasion, when a young man approached me for treatment, I asked him if he would not rather go to someone closer to his own age. To my surprise, he said 'Not at all! The last analyst I was treated by was a young woman who often wore a transparent blouse, and I found it impossible to keep my eyes off her. Not only that: I was repeatedly embarrassed by erections and I don't want to have to go through that sort of experience again. With you, at least, I'll feel safe. You're so much older than I that there isn't any real risk that I shall get sexually excited talking to you.'

I have often pointed out to would-be adolescent patients that there is not just a generation gap between us—there is a *double* generation gap. But they were not at all deterred by this. On the contrary, the double gap may be welcomed. A young woman who came to me to discuss her sexual problems pointed out that if I were younger and nearer the age of her own mother, I would be felt to be far too close to the age of her parents who had yet to solve their own sexual problems and had separated. In this connection, she confided that when she came down to breakfast, she never knew what new man she would find at the table with whom her mother had spent the night. She thought that talking to me might make it very much easier to look at such problems—those of a middle generation—together. There is, it seems, a lot to be said for being an analytic granny for some of the teenage patients.

Perhaps every age has its compensations. In the past, when I thought about my 80th birthday, it was so far off, so distant, that I thought it must be very dull to live to such an age. How boring it would be! I wondered how I would spend the time once an industrious and active life was behind me. It was a matter of very great surprise to me when, at my 80th birthday celebration, so many people, of all generations, expressed so much friendliness and appreciation of all the work we had done together in the past. But that is to speak only of fellow professionals. It is particularly gratifying that my former war babies keep so closely in touch with me and continue to show interest in me. They are now close to fifty years of age themselves. It is always a source of pleasure when former patients get in touch and if they ask me to see them or a relative of theirs; not only do I know then that my past professional life was far from wasted, but that I am still considered of use and able to help those who ask me for it.

BIBLIOGRAPHY

Bennett, I., & Hellman, I. (1951). Psychoanalytic material related to observations in early development. *Psychoanalytic Study of the Child, 6*:307–324.

Bergen, M. E. (1958). The effect of severe trauma on a four-year-old child. *Psychoanalytic Study of the Child, 13.*

Bornstein, B. (1930). Zur Psychogenese der Pseudobebilität. *Internationale Zeitschrift der Psychoanalyse, 16.*

—————— (1951). On latency. *Psychoanalytic Study of the Child, 6.*

Bornstein, B., Falstein, E., & Rank, B. (1951). Panel: Child analysis. Meeting of the American Psychoanalytical Association. Reported in *Bulletin of the American Psychoanalytical Association, 7.*

Brierley, M. (1951). *Trends in Psycho-Analysis*. London: Hogarth Press.

Burlingham, D. (1934). Mitteilungsdrang und Geständniszwang [The urge to tell and the compulsion to confess]. *Imago, 20.*

—————— (1935a). Geständniszwang und Strafbedürfnis [Compulsion to confess and need for punishment]. *Imago, 21.*

—————— (1935b). Child analysis and the mother. *Psycho-Analytical Quarterly, 4.*

_____ (1952). *Twins: A Study of Three Pairs of Identical Twins.* London: Imago.

Burlingham, D., & Freud, A. (1942). *Young Children in Wartime.* London: Allen & Unwin.

_____ (1944). *War and Children.* New York: International Universities Press.

Burlingham, D., Goldberger, A., & Lussier, A. (1955). Simultaneous analysis of mother and child. *Psychoanalytic Study of the Child, 10.*

Burlingham, D., Schnurmann, A., & Lantos, B. (1958). David and his mother [unpublished].

Coleman, R. W., Kris, E., & Provence, S. (1953). The study of variations of early parental attitudes: a preliminary report. *Psychoanalytic Study of the Child, 8.*

Deutsch, H. (1922). Über die pathologische Lüge (Pseudologia phantastica). *Internationale Zeitschrift der Psychoanalyse, 8.*

Eissler, K. R. (1950). *Psychoanalytic Study of the Child, 5.*

Frankl, L. (1965). George and his father [unpublished].

Freud, A. (1936). *The Ego and the Mechanisms of Defence.* New York: International Universities Press.

_____ (1955). The rejecting mother. Lecture given to the Child Welfare League of America.

_____ (1958). Adolescence. *Psychoanalytic Study of the Child, 13.*

_____ (1960a). Introduction to K. Levy, 'Simultaneous analysis of a mother and her adolescent daughter.' *Psychoanalytic Study of the Child, 15.*

_____ (1960b). The Child Guidance Clinic as a centre of prophylaxis and enlightenment. *Psychoanalytic Study of the Child, 15.*

Freud, A., & Burlingham, D. (1944). *Infants without Families.* New York: International Universities Press.

Freud, S. (1926). *Inhibitions, Symptoms and Anxiety. Standard Edition 20.* London: Hogarth Press.

_____ (1933). *New Introductory Lectures on Psycho-Analysis. Standard Edition 22.* London: Hogarth Press.

Geleerd, E. (1957). Some aspects of psychoanalytic technique in adolescence. *Psychoanalytic Study of the Child, 12.*

Greenacre, P. (1952). Pre-genital patterning. *International Journal of Psycho-Analysis, 33.*

_____ (1958). Early physical determinants in the development of the sense of reality. *Journal of the American Psychoanalytical Association, 6.*

Gross, A. (1936). The secret. *The Yearbook of Psychoanalysis, 8.* New York: International Universities Press.

Hellman, I., Friedmann, O., & Shepheard, E. (1960). Simultaneous analysis of mother and child. *Psychoanalytic Study of the Child, 15.*

Hellman, I., de Monchaux, C., & Ludowyk-Gyomroi, E. (1961). Simultaneous analysis of a mother and her eleven-year-old daughter [unpublished].

Hellman, I., Schnurmann, A., & Todes, C. (1970). Simultaneous analysis of a mother and her four-year-old daughter [unpublished].

Isaacs, S. (1939). Criteria for interpretation. *International Journal of Psycho-Analysis, 20.*

Lebovici, S., & McDougall, J. (1969). *Dialogue with Sammy: A Psychoanalytic Contribution to the Understanding of a Child Psychosis* (translated by J. McDougall). London: Hogarth Press.

Levy, K. (1960). Simultaneous analysis of mother and child. *Psychoanalytic Study of the Child, 15.*

Loewenstein, R. M. (1954). Some remarks on defences, autonomous ego and psycho-analytic technique. *International Journal of Psycho-Analysis, 35.*

Mahler, M. S. (1942). Pseudo-imbecility: a magic cap of invincibility. *Psycho-Analytical Quarterly, 11.*

_____ (1952). On child psychosis and schizophrenia: autistic and symbiotic infantile psychoses. *Psychoanalytic Study of the Child, 7.*

Mahler, M. S., Pine, F., & Bergmann, A. (1975). *The Psychological Birth of the Human Infant.* New York: Basic Books.

Sperling, M. (1946). Psychoanalytic study of ulcerative colitis in children. *Psycho-Analytical Quarterly, 15.*

Sprince, M. P. (1962). The development of pre-oedipal partnership between an adolescent girl and her mother. *Psychoanalytic Study of the Child, 17.*

Winnicott, D. W. (1948). Reparation in respect of the mother's organised defense. *Collected Papers.* London: Tavistock Press, 1958.

INDEX